BUYING A BUSINESS:

A Step-by-Step

for the

First-Time Buyer

by Ronald J. McGregor

THE
CRISP
SMALL BUSINESS &
ENTREPRENEURSHIP
SERIES

CREDITS

Editor: Kay Kepler

Layout/Design: University Graphics

Cover Design: Kathleen Gadway

Library of Congress 92-054373
ISBN-1-56052-166-X

INTRODUCTION TO THE SERIES

This series of books is intended to inform and assist those of you who are in the beginning stages of starting a new small business venture or who are considering such an undertaking.

It is because you are confident of your abilities that you are taking this step. These books will provide additional information and support along the way.

Not every new business will succeed. The more information you have about budgeting, cash flow management, accounts receivables, marketing and employee management, the better prepared you will be for the inevitable pitfalls.

A unique feature of the Crisp Small Business & Entrepreneurship Series is the personal involvement exercises, which give you many opportunities to immediately apply the concepts presented to your own business.

In each book in the series, these exercises take the form of "Your Turn", a checklist to confirm your understanding of the concept just presented and "Ask Yourself . . .", a series of chapter-ending questions, designed to evaluate your overall understanding or commitment.

In addition, numerous case studies are included, and each book is cross-referenced to others in the series and to other publications.

BOOKS IN THE SERIES

To Kaye, for all her love and patience

CONTENTS

CONTENTS (continued)

ABOUT THE AUTHOR   152

PREFACE

Inc. magazine recently proclaimed,". . . smart people aren't starting businesses—they're buying them." I wholeheartedly agree. The cost and risk of building a business from scratch is now beyond the reach of most entrepreneurs. Also the skills, experience and mentality required for starting a business are far different from those required for its successful management. Thus, many more people are qualified to run a business than start one. This year more than one million people like you will buy their first business.

Many people mistakenly think that buying a business requires a large sum of money for a down payment and obtaining a large bank loan. This is simply not the case. Many legitimate and commonly used ways to purchase a business require little cash, including phased buy-ins, lease management agreements,and management contracts. Many other sources of financing than banks also lend money. Ten of these will be reviewed.

Just who buys businesses today? Anyone with ambition and determination can buy a business—from hairdressers and factory workers to vice presidents and engineers. Business buyers need have only a great enthusiasm for the challenge and independence that comes from owning their own business. Age is not a limitation, either—business buyers range in age from eighteen to eighty.

One segment of the population buying more businesses than any other—"burned-out" baby boomers. These men and women have spent the last ten to twenty years working for large corporations with all their constraints and limitations. It seems that the yearning for independence within this group can no longer be constrained and they are leaving the corporate world in record numbers to start or purchase their own businesses. They want to spend the rest of their lives making money for themselves, rather than somebody else.

Another significant group of business buyers are the employees of smaller companies who buy out company founders. Such buyouts allow employees to secure their jobs for the future, while gaining greater freedom and increased income. Employees buying out their employer find that financial and technical assistance is often available from their local and state governments. Most small communities are especially concerned with job preservation and will make great efforts to help employees buy out businesses that might otherwise close and result in unemployment for its workers.

Existing business owners are also buying businesses. They do so for several reasons: to expand geographically, gain new technology, diversify their product lines and integrate their business. vertically. Business owners remember the arduous and time-consuming task of starting a business from scratch and avoid it by growing their business through the purchase of others.

The key to your successful purchase of a business is proper preparation. This book will help guide you through the entire purchase process—from locating a business for sale to closing the transaction. It will provide you with the information and insight you need to fulfill your dream of owning your own business. Do not hesitate. Be one of those one million people that will buy a business this year!

This book has been designed to help you navigate the process of buying a business in a practical and professional fashion. It has been written in a concise and easy-to-understand manner to provide you with the knowledge and insight you need to purchase a business.successfully. It contains proprietary methods and forms—developed over many years of study and practice—that will give you a special advantage over competing business buyers. You are free to reproduce these forms for your own personal use.

Buying a business is the most significant decision most people will make in their lives. It will seem overwhelming at first, but once you have read the book and analyzed a business or two, you, will be surprised how quickly you become an expert. The advice and methods provided in this book will help ensure that your purchase decision is the right one.

Before you go further, take a few moments to examine your motivation for buying a business. In the past, many people started or purchased businesses as hobbies or diversions or just as a way of not working for somebody else. A solid economy, special tax advantages and modest competition made this possible. In today's competitive marketplace, you should buy a business only if you can meet the challenge it will present. Success requires persistence, patience, self-confidence, good judgment, adaptability and a customer orientation. If you possess these traits and that special inner drive for success and recognition, then you could not have picked a better time to get into business. Today's global marketplace and the advent of advanced telecommunications and computers have created unlimited business possibilities. You can now buy and sell goods anywhere in the world. You can run a successful international business in the smallest town, or even out of your home. The opportunities are endless–so read on and get started today!

CHAPTER ONE

LOCATING
A BUSINESS
FOR SALE

CONTACTING BUSINESS OWNERS DIRECTLY

You can locate a business that is available for purchase by contacting business owners directly, contacting business service providers, using a business broker, networking within the business community, advertising and responding to business-for-sale advertisements. Each of these six approaches has its merits and limitations, and all of them should be used to some extent to ensure that all possible opportunities are discovered. Each approach is discussed separately below.

Although contacting business owners directly to determine their interest in selling their business is the most straightforward approach, it takes considerable finesse to be successful. Business owners are frequently approached by prospective purchasers, most of whom are poorly prepared or unqualified to make a purchase. This makes business owners very skeptical of would-be buyers and protective of their business. Your challenge is to distinguish yourself from those unqualified buyers.

Your approach for contacting owners of businesses that interest you should be a series of well-planned, subtle contacts, each designed to increase your credibility and familiarity with the owner as a qualified, prospective buyer. It takes time to build a trusting relationship, so you must be patient and persistent. A typical series of contacts would include the following.

Step 1. Initial Contact

Send a short letter of interest to the business owner, indicating that you will take the liberty of calling in a day or so to discuss your interest in the business. In the letter simply state that, based upon previous experience or a life-long interest, you have a keen interest in the business, and you were hoping that, by chance, it might be available for sale.

Step 2. Follow-up Call

Make the follow-up telephone call to the business owner at what would typically be a slow time of the day. Introduce yourself, referencing your letter, and, without seeming overanxious, express your interest in the possible purchase of the business. You will seldom find any owners openly expressing an interest in selling their business during your first conversation.

Regardless of any expressed interest in selling, ask for an opportunity to meet briefly in person. Most owners will grant your request. Send those owners not wishing to meet with you at this point a short letter thanking them for their time. Often this simple consideration will cause them to reconsider their decision or prompt them to refer you to another owner of a similar business who may be interested in selling.

Step 3. First Meeting

Your first meeting with a prospective seller should be brief and establish rapport. Keep the conversation personal. Learn what the owner's interests and aspirations are regarding the business. Find out if the business is a "baby" that has been nurtured for years, or just a livihood. Do not force a "yes" or "no" decision on selling the business or ask a lot of detailed questions. Often a business owner who was not thinking about selling will do so when the right buyer appears. If you force an owner to give you an answer too quickly, it will most likely be "no."

Never ask the owner for a selling price at this time or later. If you do, the amount stated will always be unrealistically high, which will make negotiating a fair price much more difficult. If the owner wants to talk about money, say, "It would be unfair of me to have you give me a price on your business at this time. Please wait and take all the time you need to assess the value of your business."

Step 4. Follow-up Letter

Send a follow-up letter thanking the business owner for the meeting. If you feel there is a basis for proceeding with a possible purchase, express your interest in doing so. If you found the owner to be truly uninterested in selling, ask about similar businesses that might be for sale. You will be surprised by how many leads you will get this way.

Step 5. Subsequent Meetings

If a mutual interest is established between you and a business owner, you will want to initiate a series of meetings that proceeds toward an analysis of the business and an agreement to sell. It is essential that you get to know the owner personally and build a sense of mutual trust and respect before you embark on any analysis of the business.

Step 6. Maintaining Contact

Since sudden circumstances (declining health, sudden financial reversal, divorce) can change an owner's interest in selling a business, you should maintain contact with owners of those businesses that interest you on a three-to-four month basis. You never know when events will change their minds and make a previously defiant business owner eager to sell. Also, a business owner who is not ready to sell will often refer you to another business owner at a later date because of your persistence and professional approach.

Finding the right business to purchase takes time, so you must be patient and careful not to become overanxious. A business bought in haste will almost always end in failure. As your network of contacts and visability with business owners grow, so will your chances of success. Your opportunity of a lifetime will probably appear when you least expect it.

Your Turn

Take time to think (to daydream) about what business to buy. Find a comfortable and quiet spot, close your eyes and let your mind wander, considering all possibilities. The most unexpected business may just turn out to be the best one for you.

Make a list of all existing businesses that you would like to own if you had the chance. Now take out your calendar and prepare a detailed schedule for contacting the owners of these businesses to see if they would be interested in selling. Don't try to do it all at once; systematically contact a select number of owners each week. Keep close track of all contacts for future reference.

OTHER METHODS

Contacting Business Service Providers

You may locate a business for sale by contacting business service providers (accountants, attorneys, consultants, insurance agents, bankers and others) in your area. Service providers are a vital source of leads because they are usually the first people business owners tell when they want to sell their business. Service providers may recommend you to a client because they feel it is time for the owner to sell (because of retirement, redeployment of assets, or estate planning purposes), and you appear to be the right kind of buyer.

Your approach to service providers should be similar to that used with business owners, and your initial objective would be the same—to build rapport and credibility. Service providers will not contact a client on your behalf unless they are convinced of your ability to purchase and operate the business. Provide them with whatever information they need to introduce you to a client. Maintain contact on a three-to-four month interval, and be patient.

Using a Business Broker

Before you consider using a broker to assist you in finding a business to purchase, you should know a few things about the profession. In most states, business brokers are real estate agents who have decided to specialize in business sales. Although many states require a business broker to be licensed as a real estate agent or broker, requirements for licensing may not include any training or testing in business brokerage. Therefore, it is incumbent upon you to investigate the ability, motivation and experience of all brokers or agents before you decide to work with them. Remember: business brokers and real estate agents are primarily salespeople. Do not expect them to be business experts.

Business brokers can act as agents for either the seller (as a listing broker) or purchaser (as a buyer's broker) of a business, and they are legally bound to represent the best interest of their client, the party paying their fee. Therefore, if you are interested in purchasing a business that a broker has listed, do not expect the broker to provide you with any negative information about the business or warn you of potential problems. The broker is charged with the duty of selling the listed business at the highest price and best terms possible for the seller. Since brokers and agents are usually paid on commission (5%–10% of the sale price) and compete with other brokers to list a business for sale, you will find that the asking prices of most listed businesses are unjustifiably high. As a result, you will usually find it more difficult to negotiate a fair price and terms for a listed business than one you locate for yourself.

If you decide to use these services, it would be wise to retain a business broker as your "buyer's broker." This will help protect your interests. Rather than paying on a commission basis— which could result in a very high fee—consider paying your broker on an hourly or fixed-fee basis, as you would your attorney or accountant. In this way you pay only for those specific services you require. Do not enter into any "exclusive" agency agreements that would limit your ability to work with other agents or locate and purchase a business on your own.

One of the key advantages to engaging the services of a buyer's broker is that an agent can represent you anonymously. This could be very important if your intentions to purchase a business could compromise your current employment situation should they become known. Also, a good business broker should have a well-established network of business contacts that will reveal opportunities more quickly than your own efforts.

Networking Within Your Community

The more people that know about your interest in purchasing a business, the greater your chance of success. You should make a conscious effort to let your friends, family, neighbors, church or club members know of your desire to buy a business. Since they already know and respect you, they will be happy to pass on your interest in buying a business to business owners they know and their friends that know other business owners. Your friends and associates can also serve as a source of character references, should the need arise.

To be effective, networking must be active and systematic. The form provided in Appendix I will help you get started and stay organized. Begin by listing in the first column each person you know, even mere acquaintances. Next determine how each person can help you. One contact might be the relative of a business owner or banker who is in a position to know when businesses come up for sale; others may meet many business owners as part of their work. List in the middle column whatever support each may be able to provide. Indicate in the last column the action you will must take to obtain the desired support. This might be as simple as making a telephone call, sending a note to ask for assistance or inviting someone out to lunch to ask for advice. Most people have little trouble with coming up with a list of 150 names or more.

It is easy to put off networking. Many of us do not like to ask for help, so you will have to set goals and force yourself to meet them. For instance, you might establish a goal of making at least three networking contacts each day. There is usually a time lag between the time you start making contacts and when you start seeing results from your networking efforts, so be persistent. Just when you are ready to give up, you will get the call that will change your life.

Networking will not only produce many leads, but it will also give you visibility within the business community. Such visibility will increase your credibility as a serious buyer and prompt greater acceptance and respect by the people you meet.

Your Turn   *Make 20 copies of the Networking Contacts form provided in Figure 1 and list at least 120 potential contacts. Methodically contact each person listed to enlist their assistance in locating a business to purchase.*

Advertising

Advertising for business opportunities is generally not very effective, but it occasionally provides a good lead. Business owners who respond to "business wanted" advertising may be desperate and have a business in serious trouble. If you are a proven business problem solver and willing to take on significant risk, then advertising might help you find a good opportunity.

Figure 1

NETWORKING CONTACTS		
NAME/RELATIONSHIP	POTENTIAL SUPPORT	ACTION REQUIRED

Whenever possible, give your name, home address and telephone number in the advertisement, rather than ask prospective business sellers to respond to a blind postal box number. This will greatly increase the response to your ad by helping to assure prospective sellers that you are a serious buyer and not a business broker or competing business owner fishing for leads or inside information. Provide enough information in your advertisement to show that you are a qualified and serious buyer. Always state that disclosures provided will be held in the strictest confidence. In addition to running the typical ad in the classified section of the paper, you may want to consider running a small display advertisement in the Sunday business section. Check with your Chamber of Commerce to see if they have a membership publication that would be appropriate for a "business wanted" ad. Other local publications that target business owners also would be a good place to run an advertisement.

Responding to Business-for-Sale Advertisements

Businesses are advertised for sale in the classified ad section of newspapers and business magazines, usually under "business opportunity" or "businesses for sale" headings. Larger businesses are likely to be advertised for sale in display ads placed in the business section of local and nearby metropolitan newspapers. Sundays are generally the best days to look for such ads. Privately held corporations doing business on a national or international scale would likely advertise their availability in *The Wall Street Journal* and *New York Times*.

While responding to business-for-sale ads is the quickest way to get started in finding a business to purchase, it is also the least effective. Openly advertising their business for sale is usually a last-resort effort by its owners, since it exposes them to possible adverse reactions by their customers, employees, suppliers, lenders and competitors Thus, most businesses you find advertised for sale will be high risk, turnaround opportunities or businesses with inflated price tags or other serious problems. Do not spend too much time on this approach. It will only divert your attention from the much more productive methods. Be very selective as to which advertisement you respond. If the owner is not immediately forthcoming with a reason for selling and the information you request, look elsewhere.

PROVIDING PERSONAL INFORMATION

Just as you will request much information from prospective sellers about their businesses, they will request information from you regarding your financial resources and managerial abilities. You should prepare yourself for such requests by developing a personal financial statement and a detailed resume. These materials should be professionally prepared, using a desktop publishing service, and clearly demonstrate your ability to purchase and manage a business. Your local library will have many reference books on preparing a resume. Outline your skills and indicate how they were successfully applied in the past.

You can obtain a form for preparing a personal financial statement from your bank. Have copies of your monthly statements available to show, but not give, the business owner to verify the information on your prepared financial statement. Attach a copy of your credit report from your local credit bureau to your personal financial statement.

Your Turn   **Prepare a personal financial statement using a form obtained from your bank as a guide. It should be professionally typed and copied to make the best impression possible on a potential seller of a business.**

OVERLOOKED OPPORTUNITIES

Prospective buyers often unnecessarily limit themselves as to the type, size and nature of businesses they will consider buying because of preconceived notions, limited experience or personal biases. They may feel certain types of businesses are demeaning or unexciting (cleaning services, for example) or beyond their capability (electronic manufacturing and the like). This should not be the case. When you start your search for a business, you should objectively review the full range of possibilities—not just those with which you are familiar.

Some of the most basic and unglamorous businesses are the ones with the greatest potential. Small local businesses offering cleaning, repair, maintenance, rental, and distribution services (upholstery and tailor shops; floor tile, garage door and fence installers; shoe and leather repair shops, etc.) generally have limited competition and enjoy steadily increasing demand. Yet many of these businesses are not aggressively or professionally marketed or managed by their owners. Buyers with corporate marketing experience can purchase such businesses and greatly expand sales and profits by installing active marketing and quality control programs. Others with broad managerial experience can buy several service businesses and consolidate them, thus achieving great increases in profitability through economies of scale. You should not overlook the opportunities within your local service industries.

Prospective business buyers with sound general management experience often avoid high-technology companies because they feel that their lack of specific technical knowledge would make it impossible for them to own and operate such a company successfully. Actually, the growth and future prospects of high-tech companies is usually limited by the lack of managerial rather than technological expertise. Many small technology companies have stagnated because their founders do not have the marketing and managerial skills necessary to move the company forward. Apple Computer might have failed were it not that its founder, Steve Jobs, hired John Sculley from Pepisco to manage the company. So don't be afraid to consider the purchase of a high technology company.

Some buyers do not consider larger businesses because they think that large companies may be too much for them to handle. However, larger businesses are often easier to purchase and operate because they are staffed by professional personnel who know how to do their jobs well and can work with minimal supervision. Usually the larger the business, the easier it is to price and close the transaction.

Businesses located far from your home may hold the greatest opportunity. While moving to a new town to buy a business is inherently risky because you face the double challenge of assimilating into a new town and business at the same time, buying a business and moving it to your hometown may have great potential. Many businesses are independent of location. Mail order businesses, design services of all kinds, business support services, informational businesses and many others can conduct their business anywhere there is a telephone. While some companies may have physical operations tied to a location, their administrative functions could still be relocated to your town. Thus, you could purchase a mail order business operating in New Jersey and move its administrative offices to your home in Michigan, leaving the warehousing and distribution operations in place. Leads for such opportunities can be found by following business-for-sale advertisements in *The Wall Street Journal* and newspapers from major metropolitan areas. You should also contact business brokers in these areas just as you would for your own area. You should be able to discern who the leading brokers are in a particular area from newspaper ads they run for the businesses they have for sale. You can get a complete listing of business brokers for a particular area by consulting the yellow pages. Your public library will have telephone books and newspapers for all major cities.

It should be noted that several traditional small businesses are headed for extinction as economies of scale and the tax code work against them and they fall prey to competition from national firms and franchises. In particular, party stores, video rental outlets and small family restaurants and motels now offer little potential. As simple and fun as these businesses may seem, they should be avoided. Bars and taverns should also be avoided because of their high liability and declining market.

PERSONAL AND FAMILY CONSIDERATIONS

Personal and family considerations can have an important affect on the final decision to purchase a particular business. Such considerations may include the strong desire to live in a particular area of the country, to have a business that revolves around your lifelong hobby or childhood dream or one that can involve your spouse and children. Such considerations should not, however, override economic and practical realities. Buying that cute little bed and breakfast inn that you have dreamed about may be personally satisfying at first, but not after it consumes your life savings and all of your time. Do not confuse buying a life style with buying a business. Buying a life style is fine, as long as you understand that is what you are doing and you can afford the time and money such a luxury requires.

Locating just the right business to purchase will take time, so you must learn to be patient, persistent and methodical in your approach. You will find, however, that your skill at buying a business will increase tremendously as you proceed with the search. You may also find that you will change your mind about the type and size of business you desire as your knowledge and confidence increases. The longer the process of finding a business takes, the more likely you are of making the right decision. Don't be tempted to make a hasty decision and buy the first business you see.

CASE STUDY

Larry Miller is frustrated with his job and the lack of future prospects with his employer and in his field in general. He is ready to make a change that will give him the personal freedom and income potential he so desires. Larry has decided that the only way to get what he really wants out of life is to own and operate his own business.

Not wanting to assume the risk of starting a business, Larry has been watching the business opportunity section of the classifieds in his local newspaper for a business to buy and has responded to a few ads. He has also stopped by several real estate offices to see what businesses they had listed for sale. None of the companies he has seen over the last two months have appealed to him. Either they were not in a business he could enjoy or they were greatly overpriced. A recent run-in with his boss has made Larry more determined than ever to buy a business, and soon. He has vowed to buy the next affordable business he sees.

Your Turn

Answer these questions:

► Is Larry's decision a wise one?

► What would you suggest he do?

Several Recommendations for Larry

Larry's decision to buy the next business that comes along is definitely a poor one, but one that many people make. One should never make a decision to buy a business out of frustration or impatience—it is a guarantee of failure.

So what should Larry do?

First he should be patient and realize that finding the right business to purchase takes time, often six to 24 months. If it were easy, everybody would be in business.

Larry should broaden his search pattern. He is now using only two methods—the two least effective methods—of locating a business for sale. He should draw up a plan for contacting business owners and their service providers directly, and network within the business community.

Once the right business is found, Larry should be ready to act quickly. He should prepare a well-organized package of personal and financial information for presentation to the owner of the business he wants to buy. This will demonstrate to the owner that Larry is a serious and qualified buyer and help move the sale along more quickly.

Larry's friends and family should be well informed of his interest in buying a business. He will need their insight and support if he is to succeed. He might not even recognize all his options.

Larry should examine the possibility of buying a business in another town. He might have to move, but he may be able to move the business instead or operate it at a distance.

ASK YOURSELF

▶ Describe your ability to network with successful business owners and professional service providers.

▶ Discuss your dedication and patience to see the search process through to the end.

▶ How will you break away from the "work-a-day" mentality and adopt an entrepreneurial outlook?

CHAPTER TWO

ANALYZING THE BUSINESS

CHOOSING PROFES- SIONAL ASSISTANCE

Although this chapter will help you analyze any prospective business, you will need to retain an accountant and attorney to assist you in the more technical areas. Working with these professionals can be a very rewarding or frustrating experience, depending on how it is approached. Working well with accountants and attorneys depends on understanding their nature and their role in the purchasing process.

Attorneys are trained as advocates. They help you "win" and your opponent "lose" a legal dispute. However, the purchase of a business is not a dispute, and an attorney taking a win/lose approach will usually kill the deal. Work with an attorney who understands that for a business purchase to be successful, it must be a win/win proposition for both buyer and seller, or both buyer and seller will lose. Since the postsale success of most businesses depends on the quality of transition assistance, it is not wise to leave the seller feeling vanquished after the sale has been concluded.

Attorneys typically are aggressive, which helps them to pursue your best interests. However, they may start making decisions that are the prerogative of their client. You should make it clear to your attorney that you will make all final decisions, with due consideration of their advice, but based on all factors involved. Remember, the risk of failure is yours, not your attorney's.

Accountants are trained to service the business owner as financial analysts and tax advisors. They are very proficient at assessing the past performance of a business, projecting its future financial trends and minimizing its tax liabilities. However, trouble often arises when an inexperienced business buyer, impressed with an accountant's grasp of the financial affairs of the business under consideration, defers to the accountant when making managerial and marketing decisions. Such decisions cannot be properly made from a financial perspective alone, but need to include all other aspects of the business. Moreover, accountants tend to be financially conservative and adverse to risk. Do not let their caution dissuade you from buying the business that you feel is right for you.

A handshake is not enough. Reach a written agreement with your accountant and attorney regarding the services they are to provide and the fees they will charge. Do not give any service provider a free hand to represent you. They should perform only the assigned tasks within clearly specified budgets.

When you work with professional service providers for the first time, you may be suprised by the size of their hourly fees. However, what you are buying is not just their time, but access to many years of training and experience. A good accountant or attorney can save you thousands of dollars with only a few hours of effort. So, when evaluating the cost of professional services, focus on results (cost savings, increased sales, reduced liability, etc.) rather than the hourly fee. Typically you will make or save at least five dollars for every dollar invested in professional services—not a bad return on investment.

Do not be shy when evaluating and selecting an attorney or accountant. Ask for references and, when appropriate, examples of work. A professional will not hesitate to provide you with this information. If you encounter resistance to your questions or are treated in a condescending manner, look elsewhere for representation. You will usually need to evaluate several practitioners before you will find one you like and with whom you feel comfortable. There should be no charge for short (thirty minute) introductory meetings with prospective service providers. Make sure you have a feeling of mutual respect with the professionals you finally select.

Your Turn   ***Make appointments with several attorneys and accountants to evaluate them as potential advisors. You should not be charged for such introductory meetings. Describe your intent to purchase a business and ask them about their experience in such matters. Request references and a fee schedule. After some careful thought, select the one with whom you feel most comfortable and have the greatest confidence.***

BUSINESS LOCATION

Property Evaluation

One of the most important attributes of business property is location. Typically, the best location for a business will be where similar businesses are already located—a gift shop downtown, a video rental store in a shopping plaza, a car dealership along the main street out of town—because consumers already shop in these areas and merchants do not have to spend precious advertising dollars attracting customers to their location.

If you are considering purchasing a business with stagnant or declining sales, make sure sales are not suffering due to a poor location. While you can improve the management and marketing of a business to increase sales, you can do little to counteract a bad location. If location is the problem and the business cannot be moved easily, do not buy the business at any price.

Many factors must be considered when you evaluate the location of a business (see the Business Property Evaluation Form in Appendix II). If you are considering a listed business, give a copy of these forms to your real estate agent or business broker to complete. A good agent or broker would already have this information assembled and available to you. Some of the most important factors to be considered include:

Traffic Count

The biggest mistake a person usually makes when evaluating automobile traffic is focusing on the quantity of traffic while overlooking its quality. Often locations with relatively high traffic counts are congested and provide little opportunity for prospective customers to observe or reach the business. Quantity and quality of traffic must be properly balanced to benefit a business.

The quality of business can be determined by observing traffic patterns at the business location during different times of day— rush hour, the midday and evening. Ask your friends to drive to the business at different times and describe what unusual traffic problems they experienced, if any. Information on traffic counts and future road changes can be obtained from the local, state or federal transportation or highway department with jurisdiction over the roadway in question.

Ease of Access

Hard-to-see entrances, tight turns, narrow driveways and poorly marked or lighted entrances will cause prospective customers to shop elsewhere. Look at your local McDonalds and 7-11s as good examples of easy access. The use of deceleration lanes, one-way traffic flow, directional signs, pavement markings, curbs and full-size parking spaces can be very important considerations.

Handicapped Access

All new buildings must provide barrier-free access, restrooms and convenient, reserved parking spaces for handicapped customers. Many older and smaller buildings have been "grandfathered"—exempted from compliance with current regulations because they were built before the passage of handicap laws. However, when such buildings are sold, remodeled or their usage altered, they must come into compliance. The Americans with Disabilities Act of 1991 requires that all businesses now make their premises accessible to disabled customers in some reasonable fashion. This may mean that you may have to bring your merchandise or service to the customer who can't fully access your building or build access ramps and elevators. For more information, consult a licensed architect or builder or call the Architectural and Transportation Barriers Compliance Board at (202) 653-7848. If you are buying an older building, be sure to factor the cost of compliance into the purchase price. It may represent 10 percent or more of the building's value.

Zoning Requirements

Always, double check the zoning for the building under consideration and have its zoning designation and authorized use documented in writing by your local zoning inspector. Often you will find that the present use of a building is out of compliance with current regulations but has been allowed to continue under a grandfathering provision of the ordinance. Such use must usually be curtailed upon the sale or alteration of the property. You must be very careful, especially when the business is in an area that has been recently rezoned. Plans for future zoning changes must also be investigated to make sure that regulations will not allow or encourage uses on adjacent properties that would be detrimental to your business.

Environmental Considerations

If the facilities you wish to lease or purchase have been used to handle, store, sell or process chemicals of any kind, an environmental survey should be undertaken to ensure that the property is not contaminated. Such a survey will be required if you are seeking a bank loan for the business. Chemical contamination is complex issue—do not attempt to address it without professional assistance. Past chemical contamination can go undetected for years or even decades, and the cost of cleanup can easily exceed the value of the property (see Environmental Site Evaluation on page 25).

Real Estate Taxes and Assessments

Assume nothing about taxes and assessments. Obtain a written statement from your local tax assessor indicating exactly what your taxes and assessments (if any) would be if you purchased the property and continued operation of the existing business. If you intend to use the property in a different way, ask the assessor if this would change the tax assessment or millage rate for the property. Also ask the assessor to identify any potential tax changes that may occur over the next five years. The only thing certain about real estate taxes is that they will go up.

Your Turn

Make copies of all the evaluation forms provided in this book and organize them in a ring notebook so you are ready to get started. Your organization and professional approach will impress any would-be seller and greatly ease the evaluation of the business.

Meet with several leading insurance brokers to determine what coverages they offer and how much time and effort will be required to insure properly the business you eventually purchase.

Obtain a copy of the Tax Guide for Small Business, Publication No. 334 from any IRS office and study it thoroughly.

Real Estate Ownership

If you purchase real estate along with a business, you should very carefully examine its title for usage restrictions, encroachments and liens. Such limitations should be revealed in a title search for the property. Make sure you completely understand any restrictions and their implications for the property and business. Take nothing for granted. Long-held properties should receive extra scrutiny, because noncompliant uses and unexercised easements are often overlooked or forgotten. Discuss your findings and plans for the property with neighboring property owners to uncover any undisclosed claims or opposition before you complete any purchase. Local zoning ordinances give neighboring property owners significant input on uses permitted on adjacent properties, so it is essential that you foster good relationships with other owners from the very beginning.

As a general rule, don't purchase the real estate at the same time as the business, because the cash required for a down payment on the real estate often limits the amount of working capital you will have to operate the business. A cash shortage could cause an unnecessary, and possibly fatal, blow as you start to revamp or expand the business. Moreover, real estate is usually a poor investment compared to the return you should receive on your investment in the business. You should ultimately receive at least a 50 perent annual return on monies invested in the business, while the money invested in the real estate will probably yield only a 10 percent to 15 percent return. The 1986 Tax Simplification Act removed many tax incentives for owning commercial real estate.

If you think that the real estate is an essential part of the business, lease it with an option to buy at a later date. A few years after the sale, if the business is going strong and the real estate is still desirable, you can simply exercise your purchase option. If the owner insists that you purchase the real estate along with the business, suggest that the property be sold separately to an investor instead. If the business is sound and your prospects are good, it should not be too difficult to get a local real estate investor to purchase the property and lease it back to you. To do this, you and the owner will have to work together to create an easy investment for the buyer of the property. If the seller is being difficult about the real estate issue, you may have to find an investor on your own to purchase the real estate from you at the same time you buy it and the business from the seller. This is called a sale-leaseback transaction, and it is commonly used. Your attorney can advise you about the mechanics of this type of transaction.

Leasing Real Estate

When leasing real estate, look carefully at the definition and ownership of leasehold improvements. Leasehold improvements are usually defined as common building elements (walls, counters, drop ceilings, lighting, flooring, etc.) permanently fixed to the property and not considered trade fixtures (safe, display fixtures and lighting, etc.) Typically, ownership of leasehold improvements revert to the building owner at the end of the lease. Obviously, the time remaining on a lease would have a great bearing on how much you would be willing to pay the business owner for previous leasehold improvements.

If the business you are purchasing leases its location from somebody other than the business owner, discuss and finalize the terms of the lease with the landlord before making a purchase offer on the business. The landlord may insist on changes in a new lease and these may significantly affect the attractiveness and value of the business. Leasehold improvements should be defined in any new lease, along with the need, if any, for landlord approval for making such improvements.

Before signing any lease, have your attorney review it. Pay close attention to the calculation of rent and its future increases, responsibilities for payment of taxes and insurance and the renewability and transferability of the lease. Ask for a clause permitting you to sublet the property at your discretion in the event that you need or want to move before the end of the lease.

Environmental Site Evaluation

Before you purchase an industrial facility or any site on which chemicals were used (especially one operated or built before 1985), you should investigate it for chemical contamination, Many business owners have purchased buildings without proper investigation, only to discover later that the mishandling of chemicals in the past has created environmental damage and public health threats for which they must now take responsibility. Environmental cleanups can be horrendously expensive—often exceeding the value of the property itself.

All facilities in which chemicals have been used should be considered contaminated until proven otherwise. Some forms of chemical contamination may be unexpected. The following checklist should help ensure that a thorough examination of the facility is made and unexpected contamination is discovered.

1. Drainage systems may be leaking or contain chemical residues, especially in sumps and clean-out ports. Simple floor drain systems may have been contaminated by accidental chemical spills, inappropriate disposal or floor and vehicle wash-downs. Drainage into dry wells could have allowed contamination to spread into the surrounding ground water.

2. Storage areas and stockrooms may contain old chemicals, which now may be stored in deteriorating or unmarked containers. Caches of now-illegal chemicals (PCBs, DDT, carbon tetrachloride, etc.) that were stockpiled many years ago are still found. Assume the worst in handling unmarked chemicals.

3. Dust and fume control systems often contain harmful chemical residues that have settled out and accumulated over a long period of time.

4. Floors and walls, especially those made of concrete or other porous materials, may be contaminated by oils, solvents and other chemicals that have soaked into their surfaces.

5. Outdoor areas may have been used to dump used solvents, spent cleaning fluids, waste oils, dirty fuel and other toxics. Look for discolored soils near back doors, graveled areas and around low spots and drainage channels.

6. Underground fuel oil, chemical or waste storage tanks may be leaking (especially if they are older than twenty years) and contaminating ground waters. Federal law requires that all underground fuel tanks be registered with the state and that those found to be leaking or unused be removed by 1994. Check with your local fire marshall for detailed requirements. Noncompliance with tank registration and disposal requirements can draw heavy fines, but financial assistance may be provided for tank removal and cleanup.

7. Above-ground storage tanks may have overflowed or leaked, contaminating surrounding soils and ground water. Remember, a little spillage every time a tank is filled can add up to hundreds of gallons of contamination over the years. Just one gallon of gasoline will contaminate 750,000 gallons of water.

8. Drainage from roof surfaces may be contaminated from fumes or dust that is ventilated from the building. Typically, roof drainage is uncontrolled and may have contaminated both surface and ground water on the site. One of the most serious cases of ground water contamination in the nation resulted from roof drainage that had been polluted with solvents emitted by exhaust fans located on the roof of a manufacturing plant. The drainage then entered the ground water through a seepage pond.

9. General site and parking lot runoff is often the source of ground and surface water contamination—witness the oily runoff from any shopping center parking lot during a rain storm. Check to see if seepage ponds are required by state and local agencies to collect, retain and treat such runoff.

10. On-site sewage and water treatment facilities may contain old chemicals and treatment wastes that are now considered hazardous waste and require special handling and disposal. The improper overuse of approved treatment chemicals can also result in environmental and public health problems.

11. Old mechanical equipment of all kinds may have reservoirs of harmful liquids (oil, antifreeze, brake or transmission, fluid) which may rust through after many years and spill their contents, possibly causing serious site contamination. All out-of-service equipment not expected to be used again should be disposed of properly or drained of any potentially dangerous fluids.

12. Asbestos causes cancer and its use is prohibited, even though itonce was mandated for fire protection. Asbestos was often used to wrap hot water and steam pipes and sprayed on walls and ceilings as fire barriers. If asbestos is present in any building you are considering buying, have it inspected by an expert. The expert should issue a formal written report stating the nature and extent of asbestos in use in the building and how it is affected by state, local and federal regulations. If asbestos must be removed or controlled, have the building owner do so before you purchase or lease the building.

13. Spillage from trucks and other vehicles often contaminates roadside areas. In addition, rain and runoff may wash pollutants into adjacent drainage systems, which may carry them long distances from the site, causing widespread contamination of surface and ground water.

The spread of ground water contamination can vary greatly in direction, speed and extent. Depending on the chemicals involved and local soil conditions, contaminants may move horizontally a few feet to thousands of feet per year. Many chemicals persist for decades or centuries.

If any signs of contamination are found or suspected in a building you are considering buying or leasing, an environmental engineering firm should be called in to perform a complete scientific investigation of the site. Such investigations are now routinely required by banks and investors before they will loan money to a business. Depending on the situation, your local health department, the Occupational Safety and Health Administration (OSHA), the United States Environmental Protection Agency (EPA) and local and state environmental agencies should be asked to investigate the site to identify any environmental or public health and safety problems, and potential permitting difficulties or site-use limitations.

Never assume anything about possible chemical contamination or health and safety risks, and do not circumvent the law. It could be the most costly mistake of your life.

PHYSICAL ASSETS

Equipment and Fixtures

The terms "equipment" and "fixtures" are frequently misunderstood. Equipment is anything used in the production of a product; fixtures are those things used to display or sell a product or service. Thus, in a bakery, a mixer is equipment, but a display counter is a fixture. In the purchase of a business, it is usually not necessary to separate these items other than for your own convenience.

When you are evaluating a business for purchase, have its owner complete the forms in Appendix III (Owned Equipment and

Fixtures) and Appendix IV (Leased Equipment and Fixtures). This form provides a consistent format for evaluating the equipment and fixtures of the business, and it will later serve as the basis for the bill of sale. This form should be signed and dated by the owner so it can serve as a warranty statement at closing. If you want to have equipment and fixtures listed on separate forms, simply cross out one or the other in the title of the form.

Business equipment and fixtures are often leased, so be very careful to distinguish between leased and owned equipment. You do not want to learn six months after the purchase that a piece of equipment you purchased was actually leased and is owned by somebody else.

Just because a business happens to own or lease a certain amount of equipment or fixtures does not mean you have to purchase or transfer it in total. Many businesses have excess, outdated or underutilized equipment and fixtures. You should identify what items will be necessary to run the business and have the owner sell the remainder to other parties.

When motorized or mechanical equipment is involved in the business, have it inspected by an expert, usually a licensed builder, tradesworker or equipment supplier. Ask the expert to document the condition of each item, its remaining useful life, its technological status and its market value. Some equipment may be in fine shape, but it won't meet future quality and production standards. Such equipment should be deeply discounted or excluded from the sale altogether. You will find this to be the subject of much negotiation, but stick to your guns and do not pay for something you cannot use. If the business owner insists that you buy a piece of equipment you do not want, you may have to agree to take it to close the sale. If this should happen to you, compensate by lowering the price you will pay on other assets that have less emotional attachment for the owner.

Inventory

Probably the most difficult and time-consuming asset of a business to evaluate is its merchandise inventory. As with equipment and fixtures, not all merchandise may be desirable or owned by the business. Merchandise is often handled on a consignment or floor-plan basis, and the manufacturer retains title to the merchandise until it is sold. This arrangement enables the merchant to carry more (and sell more) inventory and the manufacturer to reduce the holding cost of inventory at the plant. Therefore it is essential that you carefully determine the ownership of all business inventory by examining the purchasing records.

Generally, when a business is bought, merchandise is purchased at the owner's cost (the price paid for an item, less rebates and discounts, plus freight). However, a certain portion of any inventory will be dated, damaged and unsaleable. These items should be excluded from the sale and sold separately by the owner through an inventory broker or by a clearance sale before you buy the business. The owner will always want you to take any undesirable merchandise at a discount, but saddling yourself with this merchandise will only take time and attention away from more important tasks after the sale.

Employees

As a business grows, its value depends more and more on the abilities and stability of its workforce. A business usually has its greatest value when its employees can run the operation without the assistance of its owner. Conversely, the more a business depends on its owner, the lesser its value. A highly profitable business could have little sale value because the owner is indispensable.

Before purchasing a business, you will want to know the function, abilities and value of each employee. To start, review all personnel documentation available from the seller: position descriptions, organizational charts, policy and procedures manuals, wage and benefit packages, safety records, performance evaluations, union contracts, and so on. This should give you a good understanding and feel for the organization.

The next step will be to interview all employees to understand their roles and determine how they will react to your purchase of the business. You will find that most sellers will initially resist your request to talk with their employees. Business owners usually feel that if the employees learn that the business is for sale, they will seek other employment. In fact, the opposite is true. In a small business, it is all but impossible to keep an owner's intentions of selling a secret. Employees won't leave if they understand what is going on, but key employees might leave out of resentment of not being trusted and informed of the owner's intentions to sell and others might resign because of a fear for their future. In this way the owner's fear becomes a self-fulfilling prophecy.

You can help the owner cope with this fear by explaining that most employees will welcome a new owner. If the seller has lost interest in the business and limited its growth, the employees could not expect much advancement or increase in pay or benefits. They will typically welcome a new, more energetic owner, who plans to expand the business and create greater opportunities for them.

As you interview employees, identify those who are key to the future success of the business. Talk frankly about your intention and what role they would play in the business after your purchase. Ask for their suggestions: You will usually gain better insight into a business from its employees than its owner. Be sure to listen more than you talk (use the Employee Interview Form in Appendix V to guide your discussions). Make sure that you fully understand the postsale intentions of key employees, and obtain written commitments from them whenever possible and appropriate.

If you are interested in purchasing a business whose employees are represented by a union, approach union officials with openness and respect. Your relationship with the union can make or break the business. Do not try to subvert union representation by purchasing only physical assets of the business. If you purchase the assets of a business and then run it in substantially the same manner, union representation legally continues. If changes in the union contract are necessary to make the business profitable after your purchase, they should be negotiated before closing.

Managers

The managers of the business should be assessed in the same manner as the employees. In addition, you will have to examine their supervisory roles and how they would work with you after the sale. Be very cautious in retaining managers who are relatives or close friends of the seller; this is typically a source of serious problems after the sale. Also, be watchful of disgruntled managers who feel that the sale of the business will deprive them of some "rights" they thought they had in the business. To avert potential transitional difficulties involving managers, clarify lines of authority and levels of responsibility and define these roles in writing. Do not keep managers in whom you do not have full confidence. Remember, nobody is indispensable. It is better to be temporarily shorthanded than to be undermined by a poor manager. Keeping an incompetent manager is the easiest way to lose the respect and dedication of the other employees.

HEALTH AND SAFETY ISSUES

Health and safety problems or violations can kill your business before it opens. If the business you are interested in uses chemicals or mechanized equipment, retain an expert to inspect the facility and review its records. If any regulatory agency has jurisdiction over the business, inquire if any regulations are pending that could affect how the business is run or whether the business has a record of health and safety violations. At the same time, see if the business carries adequate insurance against potential claims. You should also carefully review these issues with your attorney to ensure that any actual or potential health and safety liabilities are fully and properly addressed.

GOODWILL

Much of what you buy beyond the physical assets of a business is its competitive position in the marketplace, or goodwill. The goodwill of a business (or the predictable and transferable sales based on customer loyalty) is difficult to define because it is dependent on so many factors. It may result from access to special merchandise, a unique location, quality management, highly productive employees, unusually successful marketing programs, or other factors. To define the presence or absence of goodwill, you will need to talk with past, current and prospective customers. Ask them what they like and dislike about the business and what recommendations they have for its improvement. Depending upon the circumstances of the sale, you may not be able to approach customers openly. However, you can solicit opinions by posing as a customer yourself. You may also be able to approach customers under the guise of a consultant conducting a customer satisfaction and market potential survey for the owner.

Acquiring and maintaining goodwill is increasingly difficult. In the past a much higher value was placed on goodwill, because it was often based on protected sales territories, exclusive supplier arrangements, price fixing, restricted licenses, trade barriers, bidding restrictions and other anticompetitive factors. In recent years most such restrictions and protections have been eliminated, which has forced most businesses to compete in the open market—causing many old-line businesses to fail. For example, the surge in catalog sales has eliminated the hold that many small-town retailers have had on their customers. The movement of national chain stores (WalMart for example) and franchises to small-town America has increased competition and reduced the goodwill of competing stores. Computer technology and advanced telecommunications have also allowed small companies to compete effectively with much larger firms, thereby eroding their goodwill. (Section 3.0 of the Business Analysis Questionnaire in Appendix VI will help you to analyze the competitive position of prospective businesses.)

Thus, it is much harder today to justify paying for goodwill than it was just ten years ago. You should pay for goodwill only when an obvious and mutually beneficial bond exists between the business and its customers and suppliers, and the business has the resources and ability to maintain these bonds in the future.

PRODUCT LIFE CYCLES

All products and services pass through a life cycle that is driven by consumer demand, competition, technological obsolescence, fad or fashion. These life cycles may be quite brief (the pet rock lasted six months) or very long (Wheaties cereal has lasted since 1931). This life cycle concept may also extend to entire businesses when they are based upon a limited product line (such as yogurt shops) or a particular service (such as tanning salons).

Fad- or fashion-oriented products and services have much shorter life cycles than durable goods. However, fad and fashion products and services may revive and pass through a new life cycle. Barbie dolls, mini skirts, double-breasted suits and wide ties, for example, have experienced more than one life cycle. Buying a business in general decline but with several venerable products might be a great opportunity, if you have the talent to restart the life cycles of its products.

The four stages in the life cycle of products and services are introduction, growth, maturity and decline (see Figure 2).

Stage 1. Introduction

When a new product or service is first introduced, sales are low. Most consumers are "followers"; that is, they typically won't buy a new product or service until others ("innovators" and "early adopters") have bought it and have been satisfied. Innovators and early adopters are those consumers who bought VCRs for $1,400 when they were first brought to market. These consumers typically represent only 5 percent of the total market, creating slow early sales for most new products. Little or no net profit is realized in the introductory stage, because of the ammortization of development costs and the high marketing and merchandising expenditures required to launch the new product.

Stage 2. Growth

If a new product or service is well received in the marketplace, sales and profitability will grow dramatically in this stage. Profits will peak in this stage, because competition lowers prices and increases marketing and distribution expenses. Advertising expands to reach the broad market, and distribution extends to less densely populated areas in an effort to maintain market share. Sales increase as lower prices entice more and more consumers to buy.

Stage 3. Maturity

When a new product or service saturates the market, loses favor with consumers or becomes technologically obsolete, sales peak. Competition eases as most companies abandon the product or

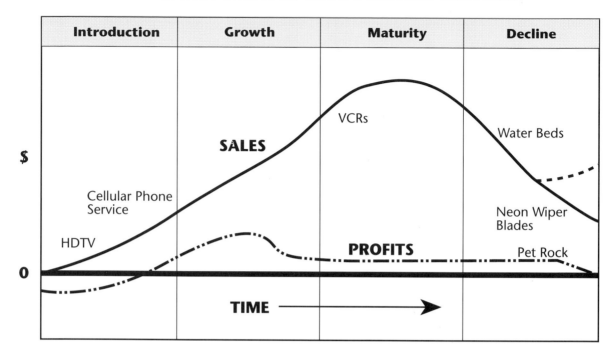

Figure 2
TYPICAL LIFE CYCLE OF PRODUCTS AND SERVICES

service in favor of more viable ones, and profitability falls to a base level. High volume/low margin-oriented companies may remain in the market, and a few others occupy narrow niches. A profit can still be made at this stage.

Stage 4. Decline

The rate of sales decline in this stage can be very rapid for a fad or fashion product or service or slower for durable goods. If the market is saturated, future sales will be the result of replacement purchases or purchases made by entrants to the market (such as newlyweds setting up a household or an entrepreneur starting a business). Sales can improve if the product is improved or moved to another market. Products in decline in a commercial market can frequently be revived by offering them to the consumer market. For example, industrial cleaners may be reformulated for home use. Exporting the product to foreign markets can also increase sales.

The key factor in a product/service life cycle is that profits typically peak long before sales. Therefore, if you purchase a business for a price based on the relatively high profit margin of the growth stage, you will soon find that you overpaid for the business. Most business buyers do not understand this relationship and will enthusiastically buy a business for a premium price just as its profitability drastically declines. Many purchased businesses fail for this reason. The ideal business would have a steady stream of products and services entering their growth phase and a mechanism for detecting and eliminating products losing their profitability.

ADDITIONAL CONSIDERATIONS

Warranty/Guarantee Liabilities

All businesses provide some form of warranty or guarantee for the products and services they sell. Such warranties and guarantees may be written, verbal, expressed or implied. As a buyer, you will want to quantify the outstanding dollar value of all warranty and guarantee liabilities facing the business and adjust for this amount in the purchase of the business. If the business has good records, you should be able to use past warranty and guarantee expenditures to calculate the amount of liability at the time of the sale. Otherwise, you may have to make assumptions based on a return of a certain percentage of items sold and an average cost to replace or repair the item. Ask the owner and all employees to prepare a list of known verbal and implied warranties and an estimate of likely expenditures to honor them.

Since it will not be possible to estimate all liabilities at the time of purchase, a certain amount of your down payment should be set aside in escrow to cover any unexpected liabilities. Such adjustments could also be handled as deductions from your monthly payments to the seller.

Proprietary Products and Information

If you are asked to purchase proprietary information or processes of the business, make sure that it is truly proprietary and necessary. Often so-called proprietary information is easily available through public or trade sources, especially such items as mailing lists and production methodology. Since the control over proprietary information within a small business is typically lax, employees (including former employees) may have it, and even competitors or casual visitors have seen it. Do not pay for what you do not need.

Patents, Copyrights and Trademarks

Patents, copyrights and trademarks provide business owners with a means of protecting their original designs, written materials and brand names. Such registrations, however, have no inherent value. The only time a patent, copyright or trademark has value is when it produces an income or competitive edge in the business. Pay for these protections only if they help produce an income or competitive advantage that the business would otherwise not achieve. Their value should be based on the current or potential revenue they generate.

Patents, copyrights and trademarks, in themselves, do not protect your designs, materials and brand names from misuse by others. They only provide you with a legal means for pursuing an offender. For example, assume you own a certain patent that provides your business with a profit of $1,000 per year. You then learn that a firm in another state is illegally using your design. You ask them to stop using your patent, but they refuse. Since you have a valid patent, you can sue the offending company. However, your attorney advises you that such a lawsuit will cost at least $30,000 and take four years to win. Clearly, it would not be a wise business decision to spend $30,000 to defend a patent creating only $1,000 in annual income. Thus, a patent, copyright or trademark provides business owners with protection when they are willing and able to initiate legal action. This is not the case for most small businesses, so be very reluctant about paying for patents, copyrights and trademarks. If you do wish to buy them, it is usually best to do so on a royalty basis, rather than a lump sum payment. In this way you pay only for the benefit you receive.

Business Relationships

Certain business relationships, such as supplier contracts, distributor agreements, franchise licenses and government authorizations, can be very valuable to a business. However, they are valuable only to the extent that they can be documented, transferred and protected. For example, a business owner may claim an exclusive access to a special supplier that gives the business a distinct competitive advantage. The owner will want to attach a significant dollar value to this arrangement. Upon examination, however, you may find that this special arrangement is based only on a handshake, which will not be honored with the new owner, or that the arrangement is not limited at all and is available to any business. Business relationships can have significant value, but only if they are transferable and easily defended. When negotiating with franchises, investigate how service territories are defined, how and for what purpose fees are assessed and what specific services are provided by the franchisor.

Financial Condition

Most owners maintain surprisingly poor financial records. You might find inaccurate, incomplete and unverifiable records or even two sets of books—one for the business owner and another for the Internal Revenue Service. Your task will be to examine these financial records and project how the business will do under your ownership. The basic documents you will want to obtain from the seller are:

- ► A current balance sheet
- ► Profit and loss statments for the past five years
- ► Tax returns for the past five years
- ► Schedules of accounts receivable and payable

- ► Copies of any audits or financial analyses
- ► Dun and Bradstreet listing
- ► Sales, use, withholding and unemployment tax reports for the past three years
- ► Any other available financial documents

Review all financial documents that exist. You will need the assistance of your accountant to analyze and reconstruct these records. Some business owners may be hesitant about sharing their financial records with you and may ask you to sign a confidentiality agreement. Sign the agreement and assure the owner that you understand their reservations and that you will properly handle all information provided to you.

In addition to the information provided by the seller, public information on the business is available in the form of UCC-1 (Universal Commercial Code) filing and annual corporate reports. A UCC-1 filing is filed by creditors of a business with the secretary of state and local registrar of deeds to alert the public to a debt owed by a business and the collateral pledged. By filing a UCC-11 form with the secretary of state you can obtain copies of all UCC-1 form on file for a particular business.

All incorporated businesses must file an annual corporate report with the secretary of state of the state in which they are incorporated. This contains a balance sheet for the business and a statement of ownership. Annual reports are public documents and copies can be obtained by anyone from the state for a small fee. Your accountant or attorney can help you request copies of annual reports.

Almost every type of business is represented by some sort of trade association. These associations can provide a wealth of helpful information, such as financial summaries, ratio analyses, market trends and supplier and vendor lists. The trade associations representing the industry you are interested in can be found in the *Encyclopedia of Associations*, which is available in the reference section of most libraries. The reference librarian can help you obtain other useful information on particular businesses or industries. In addition, the commercial loan officer at your bank will have access to additional reference sources that could be beneficial. Do not be afraid to ask for such assistance. Information concerning federal income, excise and employment obligations is provided in the *Tax Guide for Small Business*, IRS Publication No. 334, which is available from any IRS office. Additional useful publications available from federal agencies are listed in Appendix VII.

Legal Actions

Most businesses sooner or later become involved in some sort of legal action. It may be a lawsuit initiated by the business to collect an overdue account, a complaint brought against the business for an alleged unlawful discharge of an employee, patent infringement, false advertising or other circumstances. It is esssential that you learn of all current, pending and past legal proceedings involving the business or its owner. Ask the owner to compile a history of all legal actions, however minor, for your attorney's review. Have your attorney conduct an independent search to verify the information provided by the owner and provide you with a written opinion as to the potential for problems or carryover liability. A pending lawsuit should not, in itself, dissuade you from considering the purchase of a business.

Insurability

Obtaining affordable insurance coverage is critical to the success of any business. Examine the business's insurance coverage and ask the owner about any past or potential insurance problems (unavailability of coverage, unaffordable rates, unreasonable deductible and exclusions, etc.). Have your own insurance agent make a complete review of all insurance requirements (public/ product liability, fire and casualty, worker's compensation, health, etc.) for the business and provide you with a comprehensive proposal for coverage. Since certain insurance rates are based on the number of years you have been in business and claims history, you should watch closely for rate changes that would take effect after you have bought the business. In some cases, increased rates could make the business undesirable for purchase.

Consult your attorney for alternative ways of providing liability protection should insurance for the business you wish to purchase be unavailable.

Organization and Use of Information

Analyzing a business generates a lot of information. If you and your advisors are to use this information effectively, it must be well organized. Use the Business Analysis Questionnaire in Appendix VI to provide a format for organizing the information gained. These forms should be photocopied and assembled in a loose-leaf notebook with tabs for each section. Once you have completed these forms and collected the information requested, provide copies to your accountant, business advisor and attorney to facilitate their analyses of the business. In this way, you and your advisors will all be operating with the same base of information and in an organized fashion.

The Business Analysis Questionnaire also contains a comprehensive list of questions that you should pose to the business owner. The answers to some questions may appear obvious, but they should be verified. For instance, the owner of a small business had been operating as a corporation for eight years and was annoyed when asked to verify this fact. It turned out that the owner had forgotten to file the required annual corporate reports with the state, and the state had revoked the corporate charter for the business six years before. Thus the business was legally a sole proprietorship and had been unknowingly operating as a corporation and filing false corporate tax returns for six years. So be tactful but persistent in your quest for information.

In your initial analysis of a business, use the Short List of Required Information (Appendix VIII) to organize your efforts. If the preliminary investigation seems unsatisfactory, continue your examination with the Business Analysis Questionnaire. Using the questionnaire will help you obtain confidential information from business owners. Referring to a printed questionnaire makes a request appear more standard or official. It will also show that you are serious and taking a professional approach to your purchase of a business.

CASE STUDY

Mary Gillette has always wanted a business of her own, and she thinks she has located the perfect one to buy. She found a local tanning salon listed for sale by a business broker. It was the first salon to open when indoor tanning became popular and it has the largest share of the market today, although six new salons have opened in the past three years. Being the first and biggest salon, the asking price seems reasonable to Mary, even though $100,000 of the $195,000 asking price is attributed to goodwill. The business has been renting its location for the past four and a half years.

Your Turn

Answer this question:

► What factors should Mary consider before making a final decision to buy the business?

Recommendations

Although the tanning salon looks like a great business to Mary, she needs to look much more closely at the business and its future prospects. Some of the questions she should ask include:

Where are tanning salons in their product life cycle? Is indoor tanning here to stay or is it a passing fad? The six new salons show that the market is expanding, but what about profitability? Will increased competition lead to destructive price wars as the market matures?

What about the health effects of indoor tanning? What is the possibility that indoor tanning will be restricted or banned because it increases the risk of skin cancer? What about the potential for liability claims from past customers?

The location of the business is obviously well-established, but is the lease renewable for a reasonable rate and length of time?

Since the business was the first in town, its equipment may be outdated when compared to that of its competition. If so, will this become a competitive disadvantage?

Goodwill has value only if it can be transferred to the new owner. What hold does the business have on its customers? Are they locked in by prepaid memberships, or can they be easily lured away by price discounts at competing salons? What is the competitive edge that creates the goodwill of the business and keeps its customers coming back? How can $100,000 for goodwill be justified when six other salons have successfully entered the market in just the past two years?

If the business is so great, why is it being sold? Does the owner foresee a downturn in business and want to sell out before profits decline? Why hasn't the business been purchased by its employees?

Should Mary buy the business? Probably not. There is too much potential for competitive price slashing and future liability claims. The profitability of the industry has probably peaked because of increasing competition and the need to update equipment continually. The industry will probably consolidate into a few national chains and franchises, which will squeeze out most of the locally owned salons. This has happened to party stores, motels and gas stations in recent years.

ASK YOURSELF

► How can your accountant help you to analyze the opportunity?

► Who else should you rely on?

► Identify the skills necessary to analyze a business properly for purchase. Compare your skills to those you have identified.

CHAPTER
THREE

ESTABLISHING
FAIR MARKET
VALUE

METHODS FOR EVALUAT- ING FAIR MARKET VALUE

Do not believe that a simple formula can establish the fair market value of a business. Ultimately, the value of a business is what a buyer agrees to pay and a seller is willing to accept. The value of a business can vary weekly, depending upon interest rates, strength of the economy, availability of capital, sales prospects and other factors. Witness the value of United Airline stock, which varied between $95 and $298 per share from 1988 to 1990, as various prospective buyers attempted to purchase the company.

Only two approaches to valuing the typical small business are credible: replacement cost and return on investment.

REPLACEMENT COST

The replacement cost method attempts to calculate what it would take to replace a business in kind (acquiring a similar location, product lines, sales levels, profitability and so on). The cost of acquiring comparable tangible assets (inventory, fixtures, equipment) is quite easy to determine by working with suppliers and vendors, but calculating the cost of replacing a customer basc, name recognition and other intangible assets is more difficult. The cost of creating comparable sales can be estimated by developing an advertising and promotion program adequate to achieve the desired level of sales. The estimated operating loses during the start-up period would approximate the goodwill value of most businesses. When this value is added to the cost of duplicating the tangible assets, an approximate cost of business replacement is found. Thus, if you expected to take twelve months to achieve a sales level similar to that of the business in question and incur an operating loss of $35,000 while doing so, the goodwill value of the business would be about $35,000. Assuming the cost of duplicating the physical assets of the business is $120,000, a fair purchase price would be about $155,000.

Obviously, the actual calculation of the replacement cost for a particular business will be more complicated and require the development of a complete business plan (see Appendix IX). If the business you are interested in purchasing has had a history of poor customer service or outdated facilities, it might be easy to attract its customers by setting up a competing business nearby. Use the real possibility of starting up a competing business to negotiate a more reasonable price. Explain to the owners that you are truly committed to owning a business like theirs and if you cannot purchase their business at an equitable price, you intend to open a competing business nearby.

RETURN ON INVESTMENT

The return on investment approach compares the potential rate of income generation of the business with that of other possible investments (stocks, bonds, etc.). A risk/reward relationship is established to determine an appropriate return on investment for the business in question. For instance, if you have been achieving an 18 percent annual return from investing in blue-chip stocks, you would expect to earn a higher rate of return when purchasing an inherently more risky small business. Typically, you would want a total annual return on your investment (a combination of interest paid, if any, and appreciation in value of business) of at least 25 percent for a relatively stable and predictable business, and much more for a business with significant inherent risks. Thus, if a business could generate a net cash flow of $50,000 per year, you, expecting a 25 percent annual return, would value the business at $200,000 ($50,000 divided by 25 percent).

Pricing a business in this manner assumes that it is purchased for cash, inventory is purchased separately at cost, real estate is leased at a fair market rate and the owner's draws, wages, benefits and perks are appropriate for the work performed. The assumption of a cash purchase is for calculation purposes only; in actuality, you would want to purchase the business on terms. To price a business this way, you would have to reconstruct the profit and loss statement to reflect your ownership of the business—each line item for sales and expenditures would be restated. The Operating Statement form (see page 49) will assist you in this task. Sales must be adjusted to reflect "normal," expected earnings. The sale of capital assets, large, one-time sales and significant sales from major contracts about to expire must be excluded from future sales projections to make them realistic. Also, funds must be allocated to correct damage caused by deferred maintenance. Prorate future capital expenditures for expected roof repair, parking lot repaving, equipment replacement and other work that should have been prevented or delayed through proper maintenance.

Figure 3

OPERATING STATEMENT

Period of _____

Distribution of Sales	CURRENT PERIOD	PERIOD LAST YEAR	YEAR TO DATE	YTD LAST YEAR
_____ _____ _____	$ _____	$ _____	$ _____	$ _____
Total Sales	_____ (*)	_____ ( )	_____ ( )	_____ ( )
Cost of Goods Sold	_____ ( )	_____ ( )	_____ ( )	_____ ( )
Gross Profit	_____ ( )	_____ ( )	_____ ( )	_____ ( )
Operating Expenses				
Personnel	_____ ( )	_____ ( )	_____ ( )	_____ ( )
Marketing	_____ ( )	_____ ( )	_____ ( )	_____ ( )
Occupation Costs	_____ ( )	_____ ( )	_____ ( )	_____ ( )
Travel and Entertainment	_____ ( )	_____ ( )	_____ ( )	_____ ( )
Communications	_____ ( )	_____ ( )	_____ ( )	_____ ( )
Depreciation	_____ ( )	_____ ( )	_____ ( )	_____ ( )
Other	_____ ( )	_____ ( )	_____ ( )	_____ ( )
Total Operating Expense	_____ ( )	_____ ( )	_____ ( )	_____ ( )
Misc. Income (Expense)	_____ ( )	_____ ( )	_____ ( )	_____ ( )
NET OPERATING PROFIT	_____ ( )	_____ ( )	_____ ( )	_____ ( )
Debt Service	_____ ( )	_____ ( )	_____ ( )	_____ ( )
Owners Draw	_____ ( )	_____ ( )	_____ ( )	_____ ( )
NET INCOME	_____ ( )	_____ ( )	_____ ( )	_____ ( )

*% of Sales

Figure 4

CASH FLOW PROJECTION

INCOME/EXPENSE	Plan	Actual	Plan	Actual	Plan	Actual
CASH RECEIPTS						
1. Cash Sales						
2. Payments on Accounts						
3. Other Income						
4. TOTAL CASH RECEIPTS						
PLANNED CASH PAYMENTS						
5. Inventory						
6. Wages						
7. Utilities						
8. Rent						
9. Maintenance						
10. Insurance						
11. Debt Service						
12. Office Expenses						
13. Advertising						
14. Taxes and Fees						
15. Freight						
16. Professional Services						
17. Other Services						
18. _____						
19. _____						
20. _____						
21. Owner's Draw						
22. TOTAL CASH PAYMENTS						
CASH BALANCES						
23. Cash at Beginning of Month						
24. Cash Change: Item 4-22						
25. CASH AT END OF MONTH						

Once the profit-and-loss statement has been reconstructed to reflect your ownership and proper operation of the business, make a cash flow projection (see the Cash Flow Projection form on page 50). The cash flow projection will show whether the business will experience negative cash flow (most newly purchased businesses do) after your purchase and allow you to calculate the amount of cash (working capital) you will need to operate the business initially. The greater the working capital requirement, the greater the risk of operation and less the overall value of the business. A high working capital requirement mandates a much lower cash down payment for the business to balance the risks between you and the seller.

Since so many intricacies are involved in the valuation of a business using the return on investment approach, you will need the assistance of your accountant to complete this analysis. Neither of these pricing methods should be used in an absolute fashion. In the end, your offering price will be based on a combination of your analysis and business intuition. The matter of arriving at an appropriate offering price will seem overwhelming at first, but after you have had an opportunity to evaluate a few prospective businesses, you will become more proficient at valuing a business.

Other Methods of Valuation

Sellers might want to value their business using a rule of thumb, or income multiplier. This method derives a value for a business by multiplying the income of the business by some accepted factor for the industry. For example, a small motel in a prime location might be valued by multiplying its gross income by a factor of five. Thus, a small motel with an annual gross income of $100,000 would be valued at $500,000. The difficulty with this approach is that it does not fully consider differences in the quality of business assets. Consider the example of twin motels sitting side by side, built exactly the same twenty-five years ago. Each has a gross income of $100,000. The assumption, using an income multiple of five, is that each is worth $500,000. However, one motel has just had a new $50,000 roof installed, while the roof of the other motel is ready to start leaking. Are they both worth $500,000 as the rule of thumb suggests? Obviously not. The second motel is worth $450,000 because of the need to spend $50,000 on a new roof. Rules of thumb should therefore not be used for anything more than estimating the value of a business. Many business brokers and other professionals use the income multiplier approach, but it is only the easiest, not the best way to calculate the value of a business.

Another approach to valuation is that of comparable sales. In residential real estate the use of the comparable sales approach has merit. If the last six three-bedroom ranch homes sold in your neighborhood for an average of $75,000, then your three-bedroom ranch is probably worth approximately $75,000, allowing for differences such as swimming pools and the like. The problem with using comparable sales with businesses is finding any that are reasonably comparable. Businesses within the same industry can vary significantly in many ways—location, profitability, customer base, contractual obligations and asset ownership are some of the most critical factors. Thus, two businesses in the same town, similar in size and sales, may differ in value by more than 100 percent.

Using Appraisers

You may wish to use an appraiser to help value the business you wish to buy. Real estate brokers, state licensed appraisers, accountants and other business advisors may offer appraisal services. In the past it was fairly easy for these professionals to appraise the value of a business. The value of most businesses was largely represented by hard assets such as buildings, inventory and equipment, which have an active resale market, and businesses generally experienced steady growth along with the economy. But today's businesses often lease their facilities and equipment, maintain minimal standing inventory and have fluctuating sales and profitability. These conditions make obsolete the simple formulas used by most appraisers in the past. Most appraisers appreciate neither the dynamics of today's businesses nor the ephemeral nature of goodwill, which causes them often to grossly overstate the goodwill value of businesses. It is probably best to use appraisers only to determine the current market value of specific hard assets for which they have a recognized expertise. Rely on your own judgment to evaluate goodwill and other intangible assets.

Tax Considerations

Once you arrive at what you think is a fair cash value for a business, the final step is working with your accountant to structure your offer in such a way as to give you the best overall tax advantages and least financial risk. Since you will almost never pay cash for a business, the amount of down payment, interest rate and term of the note taken back by the seller will all affect the final price paid for the business. For instance, if the owner demanded a large down payment and high interest rate on the note, the final amount paid for the business would be reduced to adjust for your higher initial investment and subsequent risk. If, on the other hand, the owner prefers a longer-term note and only a modest down payment (to defer the income from the sale to future tax years, for instance), the final price would be somewhat higher because of your reduced initial investment and overall risk. If a business is fairly priced and properly structured, its operating profits should be able to pay for the business in less than five years.

CASE STUDY

Dave Lintner is in the process of valuing a business he is interested in buying. He has found a small electrical motor repair shop that seems ideally suited to his background as an electrician. He is willing to pay four times the net profit for the business to receive a 25 percent return on his investment. The owners gave him this profit/loss statement:

Total Sales	$200,000
Cost of Goods Sold	122,000
Gross Profit	$78,000
Expenses	
Advertising	3,000
Rent	12,000
Utilities	7,000
Telephone	1,000
Professional Services	3,000
Miscellaneous	2,000
Total Expenses	($28,000)
NET PROFIT	$50,000

Answer this question:

▶ Based upon his criteria, should Dave value this business at $250,000?

Recommendations

Dave should not value this business at $200,000. The owners' net profit figure does not truly represent the profitability of the business. Notice that the expense listing does not include wages. The owners did not consider themselves employees and so have not classified the draws they took from the business as wages. However, Dave will have to hire employees to do the work previously performed by the owners at an annual cost of $35,000, which will leave him will a true net profit of only $15,000. Thus, the value of the business based upon his criteria would be 4 x $15,000, or $60,000.

Confusion over what is truly the net profit of the business is very common. It is very unfortunate for business owners who plan their futures based on a false expectation of what their businesses will bring at sale. Many business owners have had to delay or forgo their retirements because of a misunderstanding over the worth of their business.

Try to remain logical, objective and unemotional throughout the valuation and negotiation process. Stay focused on the fundamentals of the business, its competitive edge and quality of personnel, and do not make simplistic extrapolations of past earnings (remember the product life cycle). Never be tempted to overpay for a business out of frustration or desperation—otherwise your dream of owning a business could become your worst nightmare. Other and better opportunities await you.

ASK YOURSELF

►Describe how you will wade through the seemingly endless stream of financial information and determine a fair price for the business you wish to buy.

►Discuss your ability to persuade owners to sell their businesses at a fair price—one that is much below what they hoped to receive.

CHAPTER FOUR

PREPARING THE PURCHASE OFFER

STRUCTURE OF THE TRANS- ACTION

The preparation and negotiation of a purchase offer is a process of meeting the objectives of both parties—balancing risks and solving problems. Since each business purchase is a unique event, you will not find a standard format to follow. To be successful, you will have to create a transaction that meets your needs as well as those of the seller—a win-win proposition. This will often seem an impossible task, but with perseverance and objectivity you will succeed.

Once you have found an attractive business and the owner has agreed to entertain your offer to purchase, try to ascertain the goals of both parties. Begin by listing your reasons for wanting to buy the business. Your reasons may be the desire for independence, financial reward, ability to live in a particular town, fulfillment of a lifelong dream or other factors. Next you will want to list the objectives of the seller. These may be to raise cash for unexpected personal needs, a desire to retire, an opportunity for change or financial gain. It is the fulfillment of these basic desires that will drive the preparation of a purchase offer acceptable to both parties. So take time to understand your motivations and those of the seller.

As you structure the transaction, problems and risks will arise that could prevent the purchase of the business. For example, the owner may want a large sum of money immediately upon sale but you have only a small amount of cash set aside for a down payment, or the owner wants you to purchase a large inventory of merchandise for cash but its saleability is suspect. Finding solutions to such problems is limited only by your imagination, persistence and good business sense.

Some of the typical ways of structuring a business transaction to meet the particular objectives of the buyer and seller and addressing commonly encountered problems include:

Outright Purchase

In this case, an owner sells the business for cash or a combination of a cash down payment and a promissory note carried back by the seller. The title to the assets of the business passes to the purchaser at the time of sale. This type of purchase is typically used when a transaction is relatively straightforward and without significant lingering risks for either party. A cash purchase or one with a generous cash downpayment from a well-qualified buyer leaves little postsale risk for the seller. The buyer, limiting the seller's risk, can obtain the lowest price possible for the business.

Avoid purchasing a business for cash, regardless of the size of the transaction or your ability to pay. Once you have paid cash to a seller you have severely limited your effective recourse should you discover after the sale that you are responsible for some undisclosed liability of the seller. If you still owed the seller a substantial amount of money, you would have a much easier time recovering the amount of the undisclosed liability. More-over, sellers, knowing that they will be carrying a note after the sale, tend to be more forthcomlng about the intricacies of the business and concerned with its success under your ownership.

Phased-In Purchase

The sale of a business that is bought a portion at a time, with the buyer usually acquiring the entire business within three to five years, is called a phased-in purchase. This approach is commonly used to resolve the problem of the buyer lacking adequate cash to make an outright purchase. A phased-in purchase helps reduce the owner's risk of accepting a small down payment, because the title passes to the purchaser only as installments are paid; in an outright purchase the owner transfers title to the entire business at the time of sale. Should the buyer default, the owner is faced with recovering only those assets for which title has already passed, to compensate for any loss. The phased-in approach also lets the owner easily regain control over the operation of the business, thus further limiting any losses from a buyer's default.

Lease Management

Under a lease management approach, the buyer does not initially purchase assets of the business, but pays the owner a monthly fee for the right to operate the business. The prospective pur-chaser also acquires the option to purchase the business at a later date for a specified price and terms. Depending upon the type of business involved, the purchaser may buy the current inventory of the business or sell it on consignment for the owner.

The lease management approach is another way to address a buyer's lack of an adequate cash down payment for an outright purchase, but more often, it is used to alleviate a buyer's concerns over the future prospects and liabilities of the business. Many small business owners maintain poor financial records and fail to document important business relationships in written contracts and agreements. A business may seem profitable, but the prospective buyer is taking a risk because the company's financial prospects cannot be verified. By leasing the business flrst, the buyer will have time to witness the actual operation of the business before assuming the risk of its purchase.

The lease management approach is especially useful in a turnaround situation, where the risks are high (as well as the potential rewards), and all available cash is needed for saving the business. Leasing a business also gives a cash poor or inexperienced buyer time to raise funds for the purchase. A lender would consider a buyer who had successfully operated the business for several years and substantially increased its value (creating a lower loan-to-equity ratio for the lender) to be a much better risk.

Marketing Agreement

If you are considering purchasing a manufacturing concern because you think that you could better market its products, you may want to consider using a marketing agreement instead. A marketing agreement is a long-term contract with a company that gives you the exclusive right to market and sell its products within a particular geographic territory or customer base. If your skills are in sales, why buy the entire company—and assume the burden of manufacturing—when a marketing agreement would allow you to concentrate your funds and efforts in your area of greatest expertise?

Any company providing you with exclusive rights to sell its product in a particular market would require you to meet strict performance standards. Clarify all such agreements in writing. Be especially certain about how sales to national companies with outlets in your marketing territory would be handled.

Licensing Contracts

If your principal motivation for buying a business is to manufacture or distribute a product you have developed, you may wish to consider a licensing contract as an alternative to purchase. Under a licensing contract, a company agrees to manufacture and distribute your product along with its own. You have the advantage of having your product identified with an established trade name and distributed through an existing sales network. The participating company has the benefit of product line extension without the need to undertake an expensive research and development effort—a win-win situation.

Management Contract

Under a management contract, the prospective buyer initially manages the operation of the business for the owner on a fee basis and later, if things go well, exercises an option to buy the business. This arrangement is generally used in a turnaround situation, where the prospective buyer has the managerial expertise to rescue the business but is unwilling or unable to purchase the business under current circumstances and the owner is at great risk of losing the business altogether.

Usually the creditors and lenders to the business will be happy to work with a qualified buyer, because they hope to collect the monies owed them. Once the turnaround is completed, the value of the business should be much greater than the original option price, providing a substantial capital gain for the buyer and avoiding a complete loss for the seller.

Any management contract should be very specific as to the duties, responsibilities and authority of both parties. Procedures for the receipt, control and disbursement of funds will obviously require special attention, as will plans for capital improvements and inventory expansion.

FINANCING ALTERNATIVES

Most prospective buyers do not have the cash to purchase a business outright. Even if you could afford to pay cash for a business, you should consider outside financing as a way of spreading your risk and increasing your return on investment.

The seller should be the primary source of financing, usually holding a note for at least 70 percent of the purchase price. Other potential sources of financing include banks, investors, employees, suppliers, customers, landlord, government agencies, business broker, tenants, spin-offs and family members. Consult your attorney and accountant before embarking on any form of financing. Note that each state has usury laws that limit the amount of interest that can be charged under different circumstances, and the IRS sets minimum interest rates on personal loans for income tax purposes. No one source of financing is necessarily better than another; each has its own benefits and risks.

Seller Financing

Financing provided by the seller of the business should be the least expensive and require the least collateral from the buyer, because the seller is the most knowledgeable party involved in the transaction and would have the easiest time recovering from a default. The seller also has the most to gain from the sale of the business.

Generally the interest rate for seller financing would be one or two points over prime rate. The term of the loan is usually three to five years; the loan could be amortized over a longer period, say twenty to twenty-five years, with a balloon payment after three to five years. Do not give any personal guarantees for repayment, pledging only purchased assets as collateral. Occasionally, limited personal guarantees will be necessary and appropriate, but your spouse should never provide a personal guarantee. Otherwise all of your jointly held personal assets (home, personal property, etc.) would be at risk should the business fail.

Personal Financing

If your cash savings prove inadequate, you may have to utilize some of your personal credit lines to obtain the money necessary to buy a business. Sources of personal credit might include cash advances on your credit cards, loans through your investment account at your stockbroker, loans against the cash value built up in your life insurance policies, home equity loans or second mortgages, sale of assets (boats, snowmobiles, etc.) or sale of collectibles (stamp, coin and art collections, loans from retirement accounts).

Before using any of these sources of personal credit, you must be thoroughly convinced of the viability of the business you are about to purchase. You should never commit all of your personal resources. Maintain a substantial amount as a cash reserve and emergency fund. Ideally, you should set aside enough money to live on for the first year without having to take any money out of the business. Otherwise, money worries could sabotage the success of your new business and your personal life.

Bank Financing

Business buyers have great trouble convincing banks to loan funds for the purchase of a business (unless the buyer is very strong financially), because banks are organized as low-risk collateral lenders. Generally, the collateral used to secure a loan must be liquid and intrinsically valuable; that is, easily attached and sold for the amount owed. This is usually the case for single-family homes but not for business assets, which often bring only cents on the dollar when liquidated during a foreclosure.

Thus, when lending money for the purchase of a business, a bank will usually require you to pledge additional collateral, offer personal guarantees or provide a financially strong cosigner or guarantor. If you can meet these conditions, a bank will finance a loan at an interest rate lower than that available from any source other than the seller.

Investor Financing

Most communities have professional investment firms and private investors who are interested in funding business purchases in return for a high yield. Typically, these investors are willing to invest in a business purchase without requiring the buyer to place personal assets at risk in return for a yield much higher than that expected by banks. Since a newly purchased business often cannot afford to pay the higher interest rates desired by the investor, part of the investor's return is usually provided through some sharing of ownership or future profits.

In this way, an investor can provide the needed funds at low rates and still achieve an expected high return on investment through sharing of future profits or sale of ownership interests. Obviously, any such agreement must be spelled out in writing and reviewed by your attorney.

Whenever you enter into a financial agreement with a private investor, always include a buyout clause and a cap on profit sharing. Otherwise you may find that after all your long hours and hard work, your investor is making an excessive profit on what might have been a relatively small and risk-free investment.

Employee Financing

Depending on the type of business and its location, you may find that the employees might be interested in helping finance your purchase of the business as a way of preserving their jobs and profiting from the business's future growth. Their financial assistance could be in the form of cash contributions, loans, stock purchases, equipment purchase and leaseback to the business or personal guarantees for bank loans. As with a private investor, employees will expect a share in ownership or profits to compensate for the risk that they assume. As a secondary benefit, employee financing will generally result in higher productivity, morale, and product and service quality, since the employees now stand to benefit from the company's greater profitability.

The business owner can realize significant tax advantages when employee financing and ownership are formalized in an Employee Stock Ownership Plan (ESOP) approved by the IRS. Since the Employee Retirement Income and Security Act of 1974 first authorized the creation of ESOPs, more than 10,000 have been formed. Check with your accountant to see if this program can be used to your advantage.

Supplier Financing

The major suppliers and sales representatives servicing the business have a great interest in its continued success and growth. If it appears that the business may close or fail if it is not sold, its suppliers and sales reps may be willing to help financially to preserve their future income from the business. Such help may be in the form of a small cash loan, free merchandise or deferred billings. Any such agreement should be clearly documented in writing.

For instance, if you purchase $100,000 worth of merchandise annually, the sales rep earns about $8,000 in commissions. Could you use that relationship to borrow the last $5,000 you need to buy the business? Probably. The risk is minimal: the rep already understands the business and would make back the loan amount in commissions in the first eight months after the purchase. The rep might even agree to forgive the loan if you agree to purchase a certain amount of merchandise in a certain time.

If you bought a similar amount of merchandise directly from the manufacturer, might that company also loan you $5,000 to preserve the account? The answer could also be yes. If your account represented marginal sales of $100,000 per year, the supplier's gross profit would be about $40,000 per year—an amount well worth taking a little risk to preserve. As with the sales rep, the supplier might forgive the loan in exchange for a long-term purchase agreement.

Both of these examples assume that the supplier and sales rep both want and need the sales provided by the business. If they sell merchandise for which demand exceeds supply, they would have little interest in helping out, since they could simply sell their goods elsewhere without making a loan or taking any risk. Thus, supplier financing will work only if there exists a mutually beneficial relationship.

Customer Financing

If your business is an essential supplier to another company, your customer may make a loan or equity investment in your business as a way of ensuring its source of future supplies on favorable and predictable terms. Joint equity ownership of businesses in vertically integrated industries is very common in Japan and it is becoming more so in the United States. It helps create mutually beneficial relationships that reduce the risk of doing business for both parties, making them more competitive.

Customers can also be convinced to prepay for goods and services in return for a sizable discount, thus giving you the cash you need now to buy the business. Be sure to adjust your future cash flow projections to reflect this arrangement.

Another approach is to create a "membership" for your business that gives customers preferential treatment in return for an upfront, nonrefundable fee. When video rental stores first appeared, many of them required customers to become members (for $25 to $50) before they could rent tapes, which allowed the owners to raise the capital they needed to purchase inventory. Such memberships are now used for health clubs, golf courses and warehouse stores for business or computer supplies, and can probably be started for almost any kind of business.

Use your imagination to create a future value for which your customers would be willing to prepay.

Family Financing

To avoid the personal problems that often accompany family financing, family members providing funds for your purchase of a business should be treated like any other investor. All agreements and expectations should be documented in writing. Never borrow funds from relatives who would be greatly harmed should you be unable to repay them on time. They should understand that the money they are providing you is risk capital and that it may be lost and not repaid.

Family financing may come in the form of personal loans, stock purchases or loan guarantees. The value and versatility of the latter option is often overlooked. Many people have well-to-do relatives who would like to help out, but they have their money tied up in other investments that would be difficult or unwise to liquidate. Their money may be invested in stocks in which they have accumulated large capital gains. If this stock were sold to finance your business, they would be faced with a large tax liability. They may also have their savings in annuities or mutual funds that have stiff penalties and tax liabilities for early withdrawals.

To avoid these penalties and tax liabilities and gain the financial assistance you need, ask your relative to cosign or guarantee a bank loan using their securities as collateral. Their investments remain undisturbed. You pay them an annual fee of 4 to 10 percent of the outstanding loan value in return for their assistance and assumption of risk.

Treat any family member who plays a role in the operation of the business the same as any other employee. Favoritism of any kind always leads to problems and may ultimately compromise the success of your business. Never give up control of the business or share decision making as a condition for receiving family financing. This will only compromise your ability to operate the business.

Government Financing

Federal, state and local business assistance programs may help you finance your purchase of a business. Depending on your location, your community may provide economic development funding, business retention loans, minority business startup grants or other assistance. To determine what programs might be available to you, contact your Chamber of Commerce, city manager or mayor, state representative, state departments of commerce or labor, private industry council and your Congressional representatives. Unfortunately, you will probably not find a single up-to-date listing of assistance, so you will have to make the effort to contact each party individually to discover all potentially beneficial programs. Many of these programs will probably be in a state of flux due to budget problems at all levels of government. Be persistent and do not be put off by the bureaucratic process you will find associated with these types of programs.

Broker Financing

If you are buying a business through a business broker who represents the seller on a commission basis, you may be able to get the broker to loan part of the commlssion back to you to facilitate your purchase of the business. A broker who does not have any other potential buyers for the business at the time might agree to this arrangement to make the sale before the listing runs out.

Landlord Financing

If the business you are purchasing is in a building that may be difficult to rent should you decide to move elsewhere, the landlord may be willing to assist you in the purchase in exchange for a long-term lease. Such assistance may be in the form of a cash loan to help you make the down payment, or deferral of rent payments for several months to improve your initial cash flow or waiver of security deposit and prepayment of last month's rent. The worst fear for a landlord today is a building standing empty, so do not be afraid to ask for this kind of financial assistance.

Tenant Financing

A business often occupies more space than it needs. It may have spread out to fill the space available, or it may now have excess warehouse space because of reduced inventories. In any case, it may be possible to rent out unneeded building, parking or storage space. By offering tenants a lower-than-average rent, you can encourage them to pay several months or even a year in advance. These funds could provide the extra cash you need to cover the purchase or help with your cash flow after the sale.

Spin-Off Financing

Many companies have vertically integrated their businesses in an effort to gain greater control over their operations; that is, become self-sufficient by performing as many support and supply services related to their core business as possible. For instance, a manufacturer may have started or purchased a trucking company to ship their products or a supply company to provide a dependable source of raw materials. However, many successful companies are focusing on their core strengths and subcontracting all other operations to more specialized firms. Thus, a computer manufacturer may only design and market its products, subcontracting the manufacturing and distribution functions to other companies.

You may be able to help finance your purchase of a business by selling (spinning off) its support operations to raise cash for a down payment or working capital. Spin-off possibilities could include the tailor shop of a clothing store, the repair shop of an hardware store, the paint shop of a auto dealer, the installation service of a drapery store or the training services of a computer store.

Noncash Payments

The down payment and loan payments for the purchase of a business do not have to be in the form of cash. The seller may be willing, and sometimes eager, to accept noncash payments such as rare coins, automobiles, real estate, guns, time-share condos, boats, lawn mowers or season tickets. Never be afraid to ask. A retiring business owner may happily accept your tangible assets, which you won't have time to use for a while anyway.

The timing of your purchase can affect financing. Almost all businesses have a peak sales season where cash flow is greater than normal—retail stores at Christmas time, motels in the summer, and so on. If you purchase a business just before its peak season, you will be able to rely on the increased cash flow to make a larger down payment in exchange for a lower price or get better terms from your investors because of the reduced risk of taking over the business. On the other hand, buying a business just after its peak season could create a great strain on your cash flow, making financing more difficult and expensive to obtain. Obviously the seller will want to enjoy the financial benefits of the peak season and sell directly afterwards, so the timing of the purchase will be a key point of negotiation.

NEGOTIATING STRATEGIES

Successful negotiation requires a results-orientated and objective attitude. An emotional, undisciplined or impatient negotiator is easily lead astray. To remain in control of negotiations, master the facts and issues at hand and make timely decisions. All else will follow.

Before you begin negotiations, clearly establish your objectives. Decide what you want to gain and what you are willing to give in return. Establish an ultimate goal (for example: purchase of the business at a fair price by a certain date) and develop several alternative ways of achieving it. Obviously, your ultimate goal and that of the seller will have to be compatible for negotiations to be successful.

Talk to the seller without the advisors of either party present. Negotiations generally proceed more easily when the parties do not feel pressured or embarrassed before their advisors, especially their attorneys. When you reach an impasse, bring in your advisors to help resolve the issue. Meeting the seller's advisors early in the evaluation process will give you the opportunity to convince them that you are qualified to purchase and run the business and that you are a fair and trustworthy person. Make it clear to them that both you and the seller can benefit and that you are not trying to take advantage of their client.

Negotiating Price

The pricing of the business should be the last issue addressed, because all other issues ultimately bear on the price of the business. It is also the most emotional issue for the seller. The price of a business must be based on its assets and ability to produce income—not the extraneous needs of the seller. Sellers are often inclined to price their business on the basis of their personal financial needs. For instance, the seller may ask for $150,000 for the business because that is the amount a condominium in Florida costs.

To arrive at a fair price, start by reviewing and agreeing to the value of all physical assets of the business. Use appraisals, original invoices or blue book listings to support your values, making it difficult for the owner to argue. Generally, 90 percent or more of the value of the business can be clarified in this manner. What remains is placing a fair value on intangibles, goodwill, patents, telephone numbers, long-term customer contracts and the like. Discuss with the owner what it would cost for you to duplicate these items in starting a new, competing business. This will help determine a realistic value for these items and encourage the seller to realize that you could greatly damage and devalue the existing business by starting a new one of your own. The final price for the business would then be the sum of the negotiated values for the physical and intangible assets.

The timing of the close of the purchase can be used to keep the seller fair and honest. Four main time pressures need to be considered: the renewal date on the building lease, the end of the main selling season, the deadline for placing major merchandise or materials orders and the end of the tax year. All of these decision points require the owner to renew personal and financial commitments to the business. For an owner ready to sell, these commitments can be onerous. Thus, if an owner refuses to compromise, indicate that you will not be able to close the sale until a date after one or more of these time pressure points has passed. This argument usually makes sellers more eager to conclude negotiations in hopes of closing the sale before additional commitments must be made to the business.

Documenting Agreement

The results of a successful negotiation for the purchase of a business will generally be documented in a letter of intent (to purchase) from the buyer to the seller, prepared by your attorney. This letter will outline the basic agreements and commitments made and specify those actions still to be undertaken in preparation for the sale (equipment appraisals and so forth). It will also indicate how and when a formal purchase offer will be submitted and the anticipated date for closing the transaction. It is extremely important that both parties rigorously fulfill their required actions and that they maintain clear and open communications. Any hesitation by the seller should be considered with alarm. Discuss with the seller any personal plans for the future to reduce sentimentality about selling the business.

Since a formal purchase offer is a complicated legal document, it must be prepared by your attorney. It should be drafted in strict accordance with the agreements reached with the seller and specified in the letter of intent. Do not put any surprises in the fine print or make assumptions—this will only damage your credibility with the seller and possibly compromise the sale. Review draft language with the seller and the seller's attorney and accountant to build consensus for approval of the final document. When carefully crafted, the final purchase offer should be accepted as a simple formality without reservation by the seller and the seller's advisors.

DRAFTING THE PURCHASE OFFER

While the purchase offer will be prepared by your attorney, it is important for you to know its basic content. A purchase offer must be carefully written because the sale of the business will be closed in strict accordance with its content. The principal elements of a purchase offer are:

Identification of the Business

Identify the business by its correct legal name. Business identities are often not what they may seem. For example, the legal identity of Joe's Bar may actually be Joe's Bar and Grill, Inc., or B & D Enterprises, dba (doing business as) Joe's Bar. Your purchase should include both the legal name and any other popular names or designations for the business.

Content of Purchase

An exhaustive list of all assets being purchased must be included (the forms in Appendixes III and IV will help provide such a listing). Anything left out is excluded from the sale. Do not overlook such things as telephone numbers, business records and files, supplier catalogs, reference materials, training manuals, off-site signs or equipment, hand tools, customer lists, trademarks, copyrights, patents, memberships, subscriptions and other important items. The condition of each item purchased should be stated and warranted by the seller. This will give you recourse should a major piece of equipment unexpectedly fail shortly after the sale.

Form of Purchase

If the business under consideration is incorporated, you could purchase the business either by acquiring its stock or buying its assets. Since the purchase of stock would expose you to past liabilities (if any) of the business, most corporations are purchased on an asset basis. However, a stock purchase may be advantageous when the business has contractual relationships that the buyer wishes to maintain but might be lost or compromised in an asset sale. Such relationships may include manufacturer's authorizations for warranty service, distribution rights, franchise agreements, licensing contracts and others. Substantial tax consequences must be considered in choosing between a stock or asset purchase, so involve both your accountant and attorney in this decision.

Price and Terms

The purchase price and terms of payment must be specified completely and clearly. State exactly how, where, when and to whom payments are to be made. Attach a loan amortization schedule for reference and recording payments and making proper tax deductions. To make sure the text is unambiguous, have an uninterested third party review and restate it to see if it says what you think it says. Clarify the language of the offer until it is absolutely clear to everybody.

Valuation of Inventory

State on what basis inventory will be valued (usually at seller's cost), what inventory will be excluded and how, when and by whom the final inventory will be taken. Generally a business is closed the day before its sale to allow time for a thorough inventory, but if the amount of merchandise and materials is relatively small it might be inventoried overnight before the day of closing. If possible, use a professional inventory firm to count the final inventory. This will eliminate potential conflict between buyer and seller (more than one sale has been cancelled after buyer and seller got into an argument during the final inventory) and provide a guaranteed tally for both parties.

Compliance with Applicable Laws

Specify all legal and regulatory requirements governing the sale of the business and how they will be fulfilled. Be cautious of any suggestion to circumvent any regulatory requirement. Remember, you will be ultimately responsible for any problems or regulatory sanctions and penalties for noncompliance.

Proration of Taxes

Indicate exactly how the proration of property taxes and assessments will take place. Be especially alert for recently implemented tax increases and assessments. Any back taxes owed should be paid in full out of the seller's proceeds from the sale of the business—usually directly from your attorney's trust account, through which all funds are being handled.

Covenant Not To Compete

A covenant not to compete is an agreement by the seller not to compete with the business for a certain length of time. To be enforceable, the covenant must be reasonable and not prevent the seller from working. Generally, covenants for more than three years in length are not upheld if contested in court. Also, reasonable consideration (usually a cash payment) must be made for the covenant to effect a valid contract.

Seller's Warranty

Have the seller warrant and guarantee all information (especially that regarding sales and profitability) on which you relied in making your decision to buy the business. If you are concerned about some points, indicate what specific recourse will be taken if certain facts prove to be in error and to your detriment. Always ask if all income shown for the business was generated by the business operations you are buying. Sometimes income from other activities is entered in the books of the business entity you are considering buying, which will give you a false idea of the income you can expect from the business. This recently happened to a young couple who bought a small restaurant without asking this question (and without any professional assistance). After the sale they found that 40 percent of the expected income did not occur because it had been previously generated by a wholesale jewelry business whose income was funneled through the books of the restaurant. The restaurant was unprofitable on its own and failed shortly thereafter. The buyers in this case also made the mistake of paying cash for the business, providing no recourse against the seller, who had moved from the state.

Recourse for Failure to Close the Sale

This section specifies the recourse available to the harmed party should the seller or buyer refuse to close the sale. For example, the seller might keep the earnest money deposit of the buyer if the buyer refuses to close, or the seller may be required to reimburse the buyer for expenses incurred in preparing for the sale (cost of appraisals, environmental survey, etc.) should the seller refuse to close the sale. To guard yourself against any substantial monetary loss should you discover a reason for not closing the sale, your earnest money deposit should be modest—just a few hundred dollars to provide valid consideration for the contact. Any earnest money provided should be held in the trust account of the seller's attorney and not given to the seller directly. Provide in writing for the return of the funds should the sale fail to close through no fault of your own.

Seller's Responsibilities Before Closing

Since the time between the seller's acceptance of the purchase offer and the closing of the sale can be several weeks or more, it is important to state what particular actions are expected from the seller during this period. For instance, the seller may be requested not to place any additional merchandise orders, hire new personnel, alter employee compensation, extend lines of credit, commit to new advertising or take any other action that would be counterproductive to the buyer. The seller should be expected to operate the business in a normal fashion and not neglect the business because of its pending sale.

Postclosing Role of Seller

The role of the seller after the sale should be clearly stated in writing. When goodwill is purchased, it usually includes the owner's fulltime assistance without pay in the operation and transfer of the business to the buyer over the first two to three weeks after the sale. Thereafter, the seller is normally compensated for any guidance and assistance as a consultant at a rate of pay equal to that of a general manager in the business.

Payment of Broker

The amount and method of payment of a real estate or business broker's fee should be clearly defined. Payment is usually made at the closing of the sale out of the cash down payment to the seller. Brokers may ask the parties to the sale to sign a waiver releasing them of responsibility for the accuracy of the information they provided and the statements and claims made by them and their clients. Do not sign such a waiver—professional brokers should be willing to stand behind their actions, especially when they receive a sizeable fee for their efforts.

Power of Attorney

Since many business owners are prompted to sell their businesses because of ill health, it is important to consider the use of a power of attorney to ensure that your purchase proceeds even in the event of the owner's death or incapacitation. A power of attomey is a legal document that empowers a person to act on the behalf of another. For example, each spouse may give the other a power of attorney to sell their jointly owned business should one die or become incompetent. Because the surviving spouse would suffer from the delayed or lost sale of the business, he or she will seldom hesitate to obtain the necessary power of attorney. Obviously, this matter must be handled tactfully so as not to offend the seller and other parties involved.

Obtain a copy of any power of attorney executed by the seller(s) to determine what limitations it may contain. Powers of attorney can be very broad—to use one's best judgment in negotiating and closing the transaction—or very specific about what price and terms to accept. Your final purchase offer would be crafted with this in mind.

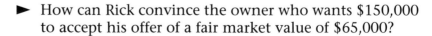

Your Turn

Ask your attorney and business broker for copies of standard provisions of purchase offers so you can review them at your leisure. This will keep you from being rushed and overwhelmed when it is time to make an actual offer.

Above all, never enter into any purchase agreement without the advice of your attorney, accountant and business advisor—no matter how simple and attractive the offer may seem. You may not know enough to know what you don't know, and this ignorance will almost always get you in trouble.

CASE STUDY

Ever since he was a child, Rick Franco has been fascinated by radio-controlled toy cars, planes and boats. He has built up quite a collection and won awards at contests and shows. Rick is well known among other hobbyists for his mastery and enthusiasm for the sport. Recently Rick received an unexpected inheritance, which has enabled him to pursue his life-long dream of owning his own hobby shop. Rick quickly made a list of all the hobby shops in his area and began contacting their owners by letter and telephone calls to express his interest in the possible purchase of their business. After several weeks, Rick made contact with a shop owner who was interested in selling his business to retire. The owner said, "For $150,000 it is all yours." When Rick asked how he had arrived at the purchase price, the shop owner said that's what he needs to purchase a condo in Florida for his retirement. Rick examined the business closely and found that the fair value for the business was only $65,000. The business had saleable inventory and usable fixtures and equipment amounting to $55,000. Rick felt that the goodwill of the business was worth an addditional $10,000.

Your Turn

Answer this question:

► How can Rick convince the owner who wants $150,000 to accept his offer of a fair market value of $65,000?

Recommendations

The dilemma facing Rick is not unusual. Most business owners inflate the price of their businesses based on extraneous personal factors. The challenge for Rick is to bring the discussion back to reality without offending the owner and eliminating the possibility of ever buying the business. Rick can pursue several strategies.

First, Rick should show the owner how the fair market value of $65,000 was reached. Often, when the logic behind the valuation is clear, an owner will agree to sell for the fair market value.

If the owner insists that the business is worth more, Rick should prepare a cash flow projection showing how the debt service required by the inflated price will cause the business to operate at a loss. Rick should ask if the owner would invest in such a business. The answer will obviously be no. Rick should then work with the owner to establish a debt service figure that allows the business to make a reasonable profit. The principal amount supported by this figure should reflect the fair market value of the business that Rick determined. If the owner remains unreasonable, Rick should explain that he is adamant about owning a hobby shop and that he will start a competing shop nearby if he is unable to purchase the owner's shop at a reasonable price. Since Rick is a well-known and respected hobbyist, the owner should realize that Rick could easily attract many customers and drastically reduce the business' profitability and value.

If the sale of the business does not allow the owner to retire in comfort, Rick could extend an offer of parttime employment. The owner may not even have to work in the store itself to make sales but could work as an independent sales agent, paid on commission. Rick could also offer the owner a slightly higher amount for the business in exchange for a reduced interest rate on the promissory note and/or an extension of its term, a smaller down payment or less collateral pledged.

Instead of buying the business, Rick could lease it on a long-term basis instead. The owner could retire on the payments and the issue of the fair market value of the business could be avoided altogether. Eventually Rick should be able to purchase the business at a fair price from the seller's estate.

Do not be discouraged if your first plan for purchasing a business doesn't work out. Strategize and compromise until you reach a solution.

ASK YOURSELF

▶ How will you purchase a business with a limited amount of cash?

▶ Describe the alternative ways to structure the purchase of a business.

▶ Discuss your strategy to assure that the seller will not negatively affect the business after the sale.

CHAPTER
FIVE

CLOSING

THE

SALE

PREPARING TO CLOSE

Closing the sale is the culmination of many long weeks of searching, investigation, analysis, planning and negotiation. It is a time of great anticipation and anxiety. You may develop "buyer's remorse." Buyer's remorse strikes when the magnitude of the actions you are about to take suddenly descends upon you, replacing your unbridled optimism and enthusiasm with tremendous fear and doubt. It often occurs in the middle of the night when you suddenly awake and ask yourself, "What in the world am I doing buying a business?"

Buyer's remorse is a very normal emotional reaction, but one that you should not let deter you from your carefully considered decision to buy a business. The best way to combat buyer's remorse is to reassure yourself that your decision was not rash or precipitous, but methodical and objective. Reexamine how purchasing the business will allow you to achieve the long-held goals that you wrote out at the beginning of this process. Talk through any lingering doubts with your family and advisors, and then get on with fulfilling your lifelong dream of owning your own business.

TYPES OF CLOSING DOCUMENTS

Closing (signing of documents and receipt and disbursement of funds) will usually be handled by your or the seller's attorney. On occasion, use of the closing services of a real estate title company may be necessary or more appropriate. Given the option, always have your attorney close the transaction. This helps you maintain better control over the transaction and allows your attorney to give you the benefit of the doubt when gray areas are encountered in preparing legal documents. Never attempt to close a business sale on your own, regardless of the size of the transaction. You will only be asking for trouble.

Many legal documents are required to close a sale properly. Some of those commonly employed are:

Bill of Sale

A bill of sale transfers title of business or personal property, just as a warranty deed transfers title of real estate. The property must be very clearly identified. Each item must be described (model and serial number, etc.) as shown on the form provided in Appendix III. A statement describing the condition of all major equipment should be prepared and included as part of the bill of sale to serve as a warranty statement by the seller. It usually is not practical to inventory and list every individual hand tool or spare part. They are usually included on the bill of sale as "all hand tools, spare parts and other items not listed elsewhere that are now present and used in the operation of the business."

Security Agreement

A security agreement documents the buyer's pledge of property as collateral for repayment of a promissory note given by the seller. It is almost identical to a real estate mortgage. You should pledge as little property as possible as collateral so the remainder can be used as collateral for another loan later, should the need arise. Do not let the seller include the statement "and all other equipment, inventory and accounts receivable acquired by the purchaser during the term of this agreement." This unrealistic requirement would make it very difficult to finance the purchase of new equipment through a bank or supplier, since it gives the seller first position in any repossession of assets or collection of accounts. Also insist on a phased release of collateral as the principal amount of the promissory note is reduced. Otherwise you may find that after you have paid down the note to $10,000, it is still secured by $100,000 in assets. This would tie up $90,000 in assets that could not be used for collateral elsewhere. It could also prevent the sale of assets, since you would not have free and clear title until the note is completely paid.

Promissory Note

A promissory note is used to define how, when and where a buyer must repay the seller for a business purchased on terms. Its requirements and conditions should be absolutely clear, especially in terms of the calculation of interest and application of payments to principal. A computer-generated repayment schedule should be made part of the note and later used to record payments made. Have your attorney or accountant advise you about the usury laws of your state and how they may legally limit the amount of interest you may be asked to pay on a promissory note.

The interest rate will vary with the purchase price of the business, amount of down payment made, expected rate of inflation and amount of the note. In negotiations each factor will have an affect on the other. For instance, if you agree to pay a price for the business that you think is too high, you would compensate by negotiating a lower interest rate or smaller down payment. Ask your accountant to calculate the net present value of each financing option so direct comparisons can be made. Make sure that there is no penalty for early repayment and that additional principal payments can be made during the course of the loan.

UCC-1 Financing Statement

The Uniform Commercial Code provides a standard (UCC-1) form that, when filed with the secretary of state and registrar of deeds by the seller, alerts the public to the fact that the buyer has pledged certain collateral for repayment of a promissory note. The purpose of a UCC-1 filing is to prevent a buyer from using the same collateral pledged to the seller as the basis for receiving a loan from another source. Make sure the language used in this filing does not extend beyond that of the security agreement itself.

Bulk Sales Affidavit

The bulk sales affidavit is a means of preventing a business owner from selling off the inventory (merchandise, materials and supplies) of the business without first paying any creditors. An owner who undertakes to sell most of the business inventory at one time (that is, in bulk), must first submit a bulk sales affidavit to the prospective purchaser. The affidavit must list all creditors of the business that have any claim to the inventory being sold and the amount they are owed. The buyer's attorney then contacts the listed creditors by registered letter, notifying them of the intended sale and the amount that the seller claims they are owed. Creditors then have ten days in which to dispute this amount; thereafter they will be unable to claim payment for any additional amount from the buyer of the inventory. Unless a buyer agrees to assume the debt owed to the seller's creditors as part of the purchase, proceeds due the seller at closing are used to satisfy all outstanding bills or claims.

Certificate of Discontinuance

A business owner who uses an assumed name to identify the business files a certificate with the county clerk to protect the name from use by others. If, as part of a purchase of a business, a buyer wishes to purchase and use the business's assumed name, the seller must file a certificate of discontinuance to free the name for acquisition by the purchaser.

DBA Certificate

To use an assumed name to identify a business legally, its owner must file a DBA certificate with the county clerk. When acquiring an existing name, a certificate of discontinuance from the seller must be filed before the new DBA certificate can be approved by the county clerk. You may also want to file DBAs for other names similar to yours to prevent any confusion or unfair competition in the future. The cost is usually only $10.00 for a five-year certificate.

A DBA protects the name of the business only on a local level. If another company has registered the name as a trademark on a state or federal level, they could prevent you from using it even though you have a valid DBA. Therefore, it is essential that you have your attorney check to see if the business name conflicts with a registered trademark before you agree to purchase it. If you feel the name of the business or that of any of its products or services is important, you should have them registered as trademarks.

Assignment of Lease

Most real estate leases allow the tenant to assign the lease to another party with prior approval of the landlord. This is called a sublet clause. If you intend to assume the lease held by the seller, you should have the seller obtain written approval from the landlord as soon as possible. The landlord might attempt to withhold approval in the hope of renegotiating a new lease at a higher rate and for a longer term. You will want to know as soon as possible if this or some other potential problem exists so that you and the seller can resolve it quickly. Otherwise, a dispute over the assumption of a lease could lead to a delay in the purchase of the business. Meet with your future landlord before closing to confirm all agreements and any changes in business operations you intend to implement.

Covenant Not To Compete

A covenant not to compete should prevent the seller from starting a new business that directly or unfairly competes with the one recently sold, but to be enforceable, a covenant cannot prevent the seller from earning a living. Covenants must be very carefully worded to achieve their desired protection. Let's say you purchased a pizzeria and the seller agrees not to locate another pizzeria within four miles of it. Later you discover the seller is delivering pizzas within a mile of your store. Is this a violation of the seller's covenant not to compete? When confronted, the seller says that the store is 4.5 miles from yours and thus in compliance with the covenant, which restricts only where the seller may sell (not deliver) pizzas. Avoid such potential problems by giving this topic extra care.

Since covenants not to compete have a limited life defined by the terms of the agreement, the amount paid can be amortized (deducted as a business expense) on a prorated basis for tax purposes. Some buyers simply include the value for the covenant with that of goodwill. Since goodwill is assumed to have perpetual value it cannot be amortized (deducted) for tax purposes. Thus, if the value of a covenant not to compete is not handled separately, you will lose a significant tax advantage.

Corporate Resolutions

A corporation is a separate legal entity, governed by its board of directors. Since the sale of the business is a major corporate action, the board of directors must agree to the sale and identify an agent to handle the sale through a corporate resolution. These formalities are required even if a corporation is owned and operated by just one person. Without a resolution, the owner of the corporation is not legally empowered to negotiate and conclude a sale of the business. Therefore, when negotiating to acquire an incorporated business, it is critical that you obtain a copy of the corporate resolution stipulating that the owner is the authorized agent of the company to negotiate and close the sale of the business. Without such a resolution, an owner of a corporation could back out of agreements made during the purchase process and refuse to complete the sale. A competing offer could easily prompt such a response, and without a corporate resolution in hand, you would be left with little recourse.

Equipment/Fixture Leases

Many businesses now lease substantial portions of their equipment and fixtures as a way to conserve capital and remain flexible in their asset allocation. All existing leases should be closely examined to determine their desirability and transferability. Address any problems with these leases early in the purchase process.

Insurance Policies

All existing insurance policies (property, medical, public and professional liability) should be closely examined for coverage, limitations and cost. Since the availability, cost and coverage of business insurance varies with the owner's intentions for the business, you must make sure that you can obtain all the insurance needed at an affordable rate. You'll be wise to shop around, both for the right agent and best coverage.

Asset Allocation

Section 1060 of the Internal Revenue Code requires that the price you pay for a business be allocated into asset classifications for tax purposes at the closing of the sale as follows:

Class I	Cash and bank accounts
Class II	CDs, stocks, bonds, etc.
Class III	All other assets, equipment, fixtures, etc.
Class IV	Goodwill, covenants and other intangible assets

Use IRS form No. 8594 to accomplish this. Ask your accountant for assistance in complying with this requirement. The asset allocation requirement was established because buyers and sellers of businesses often reported the allocation of assets differently to the IRS to minimize their tax obligations, thus reducing tax collections. This regulation attempts to close one tax loophole.

Sales, Use and Unemployment Taxes

Most states now have laws requiring the seller of a business to provide a status report on the payment of sales, use and unemployment taxes to the purchaser before the business is sold. This is done to prevent business owners from selling their businesses without paying their outstanding tax liabilities.

To prevent any unexpected tax liabilities and judgments against you for the past tax liabilities of the business, examine all tax liabilities and make sure that they are all properly discharged at closing. Accumulated tax liabilities are usually assumed by the purchaser as an adjustment against the final purchase price for the business. Should accumulated tax payments be large or past due, they would typically be paid at closing out of the seller's proceeds from the sale.

Proration of Accumulated Vacation Time and Sick Leave

If employees have been allowed to accumulate unused paid vacation time and sick leave, its monetary value must be offset by a reduction in the final purchase price for the business. Make sure that all employees discharged by the seller before closing have been properly reimbursed and that they do not expect any additional payment from you. Also determine if employees have accumulated any unpaid overtime hours for which they expect time off or pay. Resolve this issue and make any necessary monetary adjustments at closing.

General Operating Agreements

Businesses maintain operating agreements and contracts for routine services, which might include maintenance, cleaning, accounting, advertising, bill collection, trash pickup, pension administration, personnel recruiting, distribution and sales and other services. You need to review each of these arrangements and determine which you will want to continue after your purchase of the business. If any agreements need to be cancelled, have the seller do it before closing. This will help relieve you of any liability for early termination of such agreements.

Transfer of Utility Services

The formal transfer of utility services, telephone, electric, water and sewer, must be made at closing. Some agencies require nothing more than a telephone call, while others require written authorization for transfer. Deposits may have to be refunded or made before some services are transferred. If the amounts involved are relatively small, outstanding account balances are generally prorated between buyer and seller. This action eliminates the need (and cost) of attorneys' fees.

Building Access

Arrangements must be made to have the locks, access codes and security alarms for all business facilities changed immediately after closing. Make sure you get the keys for all locks. It is easy to overlook the padlock on the storage shed out back or the electrical panel until you are unable to get into it next week. Issue new keys and codes only to employees who must enter the property when you are not present. Keep a log of all persons receiving keys and codes. Notify your police and fire departments of your purchase of the business. Ask them if they have any requirements for building access during emergencies such as a posting of personnel to be called. It would be wise to ask the business liaison for both the police and fire departments to inspect the business facilities with you. They will often have great suggestions for reducing the risk of fire and theft.

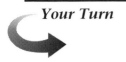
Obtain blank copies of all standard legal documents from your attorney for study. This will help you to be much better prepared for closing and give more time to discuss matters with your attorney.

The preparation of all the required documents and the closing of the sale can be a daunting task, but if you take a systematic approach and maintain control, it will go quickly and smoothly. With the assistance of your advisors, make a checklist of all documents that must be prepared and all filings that must be made before or after the closing. Assign responsibilities in writing to all parties and make frequent progress checks. Your attorney or the seller's attorney will prepare most of the closing documents. Have your attorney, rather than the seller's attorney, prepare as many of the closing documents as possible. Even though your attorney fees will be higher, the greater control you gain over the content of the documents and the final closing will be more than worth it. Have your attorney prepare a clear, step-by-step agenda to facilitate a trouble-free closing of the sale.

CASE STUDY

Things have gone well for Rita Jablonski. After many months of searching, she found the business of her dreams. Rita negotiated a fair price for the business and the seller agreed to take back a promissory note for 70 percent of the purchase price She reached an initial agreement to buy the business using a letter of intent. Later she followed up with a formal purchase agreement, which the seller signed after a few minor changes were made at the request of the seller's attorney.

Closing is scheduled to take place in a week, and the attorneys are busy preparing the required legal documents and making their final due diligence reviews. Rita has just a few things left to do. One is to pick up the insurance policy covering product liability at her agent's office. But when Rita arrived, the policy wasn't ready. Her agent had bad news. He could not persuade any underwriter to issue a product liability policy for the business she would soon own. Rita was told it had something to do with her lack of experience in the business. Since the terms of the purchase agreement clearly stated that she would obtain product liability insurance by closing and that she would maintain coverage until the promissory note to the owner was paid in full, it looks like the purchase is off.

Your Turn

Answer these questions:

► What is Rita to do?

► How can she solve this problem and proceed with the sale?

Recommendations

Last minute problems like Rita's are not uncommon. No matter how diligent you are, something always seems to come up just before closing that could ruin the whole deal. When it happens to you, stay cool. Focus on closing the transaction promptly. Don't postpone the date of closing; instead use the time pressure to force solutions to happen. There are several things Rita can do.

Rita's first step should be to learn exactly why the underwriters are denying her insurance coverage—she should ask for specific details. A simple technicality might be easily fixed. For example, the business might produce twenty products, but only one caused the denial of coverage. By understanding the underwriter's requirements, Rita may be able to make the clarifications and changes necessary to obtain the coverage she desires.

If her inexperience is indeed causing the denial of coverage, Rita may be able to remedy the problem by retaining the seller as an officer of the company until she has attained the level of experience required by the underwriters. The owner's continuing presence should resolve the question of inadequate managerial experience. Since the owner benefits from the sale of the business, any role in its management would be strictly limited and any payment would be small. If the seller is unable to assist in this fashion, another experienced party may have to be enlisted.

Rita could restructure the entire transaction. She may first have to join the business in a managerial capacity to gain the experience she needs and later exercise an option to purchase when she can

Rita may ask the seller for permission to operate the business under a self-insurance plan. She could offer to place a lump sum or percentage of monthly sales into an escrow account to cover any potential liability claims. This arrangement might assure the seller that the transaction can proceed without traditional insurance coverage.

ASK YOURSELF

► List five reasons for buying this business.

► Identify documents you will need. For each, determine whether it is accurate and complete.

CHAPTER
SIX

AFTER
THE
PURCHASE

TEN KEY STEPS

The first few weeks after your purchase of the business are critical to its success. In this time everything that you do and say has a special impact, so your actions must be very carefully considered to have the greatest positive effect. Ten key steps are listed below —take them immediately after the sale. They are designed to increase the profitability of the business and make it easier to manage. After reviewing these steps, prepare a plan of action for getting off to a good start. Whatever you do, stay in control and maintain an objective, long-term, positive perspective. Do not allow yourself to be overwhelmed by immediate demands and fall into the trap of short-sighted crisis management.

Step 1

As soon as possible, but no later than two weeks after your purchase, hold a company retreat with all employees and managers of the business. It should be held after business hours at an off-site location (hotel or resort, for instance) and planned around a nice lunch or dinner. Use the retreat to clear up any lingering misunderstandings about your purchase of the business, to articulate your plans for its future operation, and to cement your relationship with your employees by getting to know them better and encouraging their insight on your plans. Remember, your employees are the business; the quality and effectiveness of their work will dictate its success. Make it clear that you are anticipating a long and mutually rewarding relationship—one in which you will both prosper.

Step 2

Move to increase sales by having all employees and managers receive professional customer service and sales training within the first month after your purchase. Such training should be planned and scheduled before the closing of the sale. Training should focus on the acquisition and application of fundamental sales skills. It should not be just another motivational or sales hype seminar.

Step 3

Increase sales, reduce reordering times and improve customer service by providing fax and 800 number services for your business. These services are no longer luxuries but necessities for almost every business. They are now affordable by all businesses.

Step 4

Increase employee productivity and sales by changing compensation from straight hourly wages or salary to some form of incentive pay. Workers should be paid for their performance, not just time put in. Incentive pay might be commissions for sales staff, piecework for production and service personnel or base salary and performance bonus for managers. At least one-half of each employee's pay should be directly tied to individual or group performance. Incentive pay allows the employee to earn as much money as possible, while controlling overhead costs and stimulating increased sales.

Work with your employees to establish an effective incentive pay program. Once they see the opportunity for increased earnings, employees will be more receptive to the incentive pay approach.

Step 5

Most business advertising is wasted because it is poorly designed and placed. To be effective, all advertising should be professionally designed and placed according to a written plan. The use of professionals will almost always save you more than their fee, because they will be able to show you how to stretch your budget and make your advertising much more effective. You should prepare and maintain a twelve-month advertising plan. It should have a clear, central theme, a set of specific goals and provide a way to measure the results of your efforts. Advertising should be consistent, clear and continuous. Your business does not need to advertise every day, but you should develop a predictable and dependable pattern of advertising without noticeable gaps. Use highly targeted advertising, rather than mass marketing, to reach your desired customer.

Step 6

If you do not ask your satisfied customers for referrals, you are missing a tremendous opportunity to increase sales. Asking for referrals can lead to sales increases from 25 percent to 50 percent, or more. Call your customers and ask them if they know of somebody that could benefit from your goods or services. If they do, and almost everyone will, ask if you can use their name when you talk to the referred party. Call and ask for an appointment to introduce yourself and your services. Be persistent. Everyone is busy, but everyone wants to improve their business. When you explain how you can help them, they will probably agree to see you.

Step 7

Make any necessary personnel cuts and adjustments immediately (within the first week) so those remaining can get on with business. If possible, have the previous owner discharge those employees you will not need before your purchase. If you try to reduce the workforce after the sale, everybody will spend more time worrying about their jobs than working. Worse, your best employees (those that can easily find work elsewhere) might get jumpy and quit to work where they do not have to worry about their future.

Step 8

The public will give you about two weeks to make positive changes in the business. Use this time to increase sales by existing customers, bring in new customers and bring back former customers who had left because of poor service. Prepare your plan of action while you are waiting for the business to close; you will not have time after the purchase to take advantage of this special one-time opportunity. Consider some very noticeable and dramatic moves: major building renovation; new logo, signs, stationery and the like; an advertising campaign; news coverage of changes; sponsorship of a major community event or popular cause and so forth. You must do more than put an "Under New Management" sign in the window.

Step 9

Computerize as much of the business as possible starting with inventory control and purchasing. A good database will give you much better control over the business and save you a great deal of time that you can use to lead your business to greatness. Use a program that gives you real-time inventory levels and daily sales analyses. Customer accounts should be computerized as soon as possible to help your sales staff with better customer service, which will lead to increased sales.

Step 10

Adopt a "customer orientation" for your business. Put your customers at the center of the business (rather than yourself) and base all business decisions on their wants and needs. If your customers want to shop Sunday afternoons, then you stay open Sunday afternoons. If they want three items to a pack instead of six, then you give them three items to a pack, and so on. The days of closing up the shop to go fishing any time you please are long gone. It is a buyer's market, and if you don't serve your customers the way they want to be served, they will go elsewhere, and your business will suffer.

As you develop your business, new challenges will require that you develop new management skills. Some excellent reference books on business topics are listed in the bibliography. These books will help you acquire the new skills you need.

CASE STUDY

Karen Gwin has just purchased a wonderful fabric shop. It has been in business for more than twenty years and it has five full time employees. In recent years, however, the shop has declined, along with the owner's interest in the business. The sellers were in their late sixties and had lost much of their original enthusiasm for the business as health problems began to slow them down and take time away from the shop. Although several of the employees have been with the shop for many years, they have not been given much responsibility by the owners.

Karen met the major supplier of fabric to the store several weeks before closing, and they hit it off from the first moment they met. Karen's enthusiasm delighted the supplier, and he invited her to visit his plant the week after she took over the business. He wanted to show her how the fabric was manufactured and to preview the new lines. Karen is excited and impressed by this special treatment.

Your Turn

Answer this question:

► Should Karen take the trip?

Recommendations

As flattered as Karen is by the supplier's attention, she should postpone the trip for at least three weeks. She has too much to do at the store during the first two weeks to leave on a trip. The employees will be apprehensive about the change in ownership and its effect on them. They will have many questions and concerns. Karen will want to implement many changes, which will be best done by setting a good example and involving her employees. She cannot do that if she is off on a trip.

The loyal, long-time customers of the store will also want to meet its new owner and spend a little time getting to know her. This is a critical function for the new owner, especially of a fabric shop, where new business comes largely by referrals from satisfied customers.

Karen should concentrate her efforts on implementing a transition plan, which should include ample delegation of authority to trustworthy employees. This will create the time for her to take the trip to the fabric plant later without compromising the operation of the business.

ASK YOURSELF

▶ Describe your strong points that pertain to running your business.

▶ Identify the things you will change immediately; then identify the things you will change later.

▶ What do you need to learn about this business?

APPENDIXES

APPENDIX	CONTENTS
Appendix I	Networking Contacts
Appendix II	Business Property Evaluation
Appendix III	Owned Equpiment and Fixtures
Appendix IV	Leased Equipment and Fixtures
Appendix V	Employee Interview Form
Appendix VI	Business Analysis Questionnaire
Appendix VII	Useful Federal Publications
Appendix VIII	Short List of Required Information
Appendix IX	An Entrepeneur's Guide to Preparing a Successful Business Plan

NETWORKING CONTACTS		
NAME/RELATIONSHIP	POTENTIAL SUPPORT	ACTION REQUIRED

Appendix II

BUSINESS PROPERTY EVALUATION

Official Name of Bldg. _____ Common Name _____

Address _____

Lot Size (sq. ft.) _____ Building Type _____

Lot Dimensions (ft.) _____ front _____ left side _____ right side _____ back _____

Building Size (ft.) _____ x _____ No. Floors _____ Total Sq. Footage _____ Age _____

Remarks _____

Type of Construction

Exterior Walls _____

Interior Walls _____

Roof _____

Barrier Free _____ Sprinklers _____ Elevator _____ Type _____ No. _____

Appropriate for Intended Use? _____

_____

Mechanical Equipment (type, size, condition, adequacy, etc.)

Electrical_____

_____

Heating _____

_____

Air Conditioning _____

_____

Plumbing _____

_____

Rest Rooms _____

Remarks _____

_____

Site Improvements (description, condition, adequacy, etc.)

Roads/Driveways _____

_____

Parking _____

_____

Signs _____

_____

Landscaping _____

_____

Remarks _____

_____

Utilities (capacity, condition, adequacy, etc.)

Natural Gas _____

Electric _____

Water Supply _____

Storm Sewer _____

Sanitary Sewer _____

Cable _____

Remarks _____

Legal Description (from deed or survey)

_____

_____

_____

_____

_____

_____

Zoning

Current Zoning Jurisdiction

Prior Use of Property _____

_____

Current Uses Permitted by Zoning _____

_____

Permit Requirements

Current Use _____

_____

Expansion/Change in Use _____

_____

Street Description

Name _____ No. Lanes _____ Speed Limit _____ m.p.h.

Traffic Counts _____

_____

Governmental Jurisdiction _____ Surface _____

Condition _____

Dividers/Medians _____

Curb _____ No. Cuts Allowed _____

Deceleration Lane Present _____ Required _____ Width (ft.) _____ Length _____

Distance to Corner _____ Stop Light _____ Stop Sign _____ Other _____

Existing Alley _____ Type _____ Width (ft.) _____

Anticipated Changes _____

Remarks _____

_____

Tax Information

Assessed Value $ _____ Tax Rate (mils) _____ Amount $ _____

Special Assessments _____

Anticipated Tax Changes and Future Special Assessments _____

_____

Adjacent Land Use

Left _____

Right _____

Rear _____

Across _____

Other Land Uses Affecting Site _____

_____

General Remarks Regarding Condition and Adequacy of Site

_____

_____

_____

_____

_____

_____

Sketch of Building Layout

Sketch of Building Site

Sketch of Building Layout

Attachments

Last Deed Of Record _____

Latest Tax Bills _____

Latest Appraisal _____

Current Lease _____

Zoning Map _____

Survey _____

Title Abstract/Policy _____

Prepared By _____ Date _____

Appendix III

OWNED EQUIPMENT AND FIXTURES

To be included in Sale of Business

Business _____

Prepared By _____ Date _____

Description	Serial No.	Condition	Financed	By	Loan Amount	Market Value

LEASED EQUIPMENT AND FIXTURES

To be transferred in Sale of Business

Business _____

Prepared By _____ Date _____

Description	Serial No.	Condition	Lessor	Term Remaining	Payment/yr.

EMPLOYEE INTERVIEW FORM

Employee _____ Position _____ Pay _____

Yrs. with Company _____ Yrs. in Current Position _____ Supervised by _____

Notes _____

_____

1. Please identify what you feel are the major strengths and weaknesses of the company.

  Strengths

  Weaknesses

2. How can the company capitalize on its strengths and compensate for its weaknesses?

Employee _____

3. What are the major problems and challenges facing this company? How would you cope
with them?

      A.

      B.

      C.

      D.

Employee _____

4. What are the major opportunities now available to the company? How would you approach them?

      A.

      B.

      C.

      D.

5. Please identify ways in which your job could be made more productive.

Employee _____

6. What are your feelings about the impending sale of the business?

7. Other comments and suggestions:

Interview Conducted By _____ Date_____

BUSINESS ANALYSIS QUESTIONNAIRE

Legal Name of Company _____

Contact _____ Position _____

_____

Address _____

Telephone _____ Fax _____

Remarks _____

_____

_____

_____

• CONFIDENTIAL AND PRIVILEGED INFORMATION •

Table of Contents
BUSINESS ANALYSIS QUESTIONNAIRE

Section 1.0

HISTORY AND OWNERSHIP

Date of Origin _____ Location _____

Founders _____

History of Ownership

Name/Position with Company	From	To	% Owned

Form of Ownership _____ Date Originated _____

State of Incorporation _____ Type Stock _____ Shares Issued _____

_____

Related Entities _____

_____

Philosophy and Mission of Company _____

_____

_____

_____

_____

Additional Information _____

_____

_____

_____

_____

Section 2.0

BUSINESS LOCATION AND FACILITIES

Principal Place of Business

    Address _____

    Type of Building _____

    Use _____

    Owned or Leased _____If leased, from whom _____

Other Business Facilities _____

_____

Adequacy of Facilities _____

_____

Existing or Potential Zoning, Safety or Environmental Problems _____

_____

Plans for New Facilities or Renovations or Expansions of Existing Facilities _____

_____

Security Requirements — Systems in Use or Needed _____

_____

Additional Information _____

_____

_____

_____

_____

_____

Attach Business Property Analysis Form _____

Section 3.0

MARKETING AND SALES

Principal Products and Services _____

_____

_____

Dealerships or Franchises _____

_____

Typical/Key Customers _____

_____

_____

Geographic Market _____

_____

Sales History

	Year	$ Sales	Unit Sales
	19__		
	19__		
	19		
Projected	19__		

Method of Sales _____

_____

_____

_____

_____

_____

_____

_____

_____

_____

_____

Sales Training _____

_____

_____

_____

_____

_____

_____

Cost of Sales $ _____/Salesperson $ _____ Unit _____

_____

_____

_____

_____

Five Top Competitors and Market Share of Company

_____ (%)

_____ (%)

_____ (%)

_____ (%)

_____ (%)

Principal Customers and Their % of Total Company Sales

_____ (%)

_____ (%)

_____ (%)

_____ (%)

_____ (%)

Pricing Policy and Positioning _____

_____

_____

_____

_____

_____

_____

Technology Involved in Products and Services _____

_____

_____

_____

_____

_____

_____

Macroenvironmental Influences (cost of capital, consumer debt levels, new regulations, social trends, etc.) _____

_____

_____

_____

_____

_____

_____

_____

_____

_____

_____

_____

_____

_____

_____

Position of Key Products in their Life Cycles (indicate on figure below)

TYPICAL LIFE CYCLE OF PRODUCTS AND SERVICES

Introduction	Growth	Maturity	Decline

VCRs

SALES

Water Beds

$

Cellular Phone
Service

Neon Wiper
Blades

HDTV

PROFITS

Pet Rock

0

TIME ⟶

Advertising Efforts (attach recent ads) _____

_____

_____

_____

_____

_____

_____

_____

_____

_____

_____

_____

_____

_____

Patents, Copyrights, Trademarks, Logos, etc. _____

_____

_____

Summarize Previous Market Studies, Customer Surveys, etc. (attach copies) _____

_____

_____

_____

_____

_____

_____

_____

_____

Research and Development _____

_____

_____

_____

_____

_____

Warranties _____

_____

_____

_____

_____

Means of Distribution _____

_____

_____

_____

_____

_____

Public Relations Efforts _____

_____
_____
_____
_____
_____
_____
_____
_____

Potential Markets, Products and Services_____

_____
_____
_____
_____
_____
_____
_____
_____
_____
_____
_____
_____
_____

Remarks _____

_____
_____
_____
_____
_____
_____
_____
_____
_____
_____
_____
_____
_____

Section 4.0

PRODUCTION AND MANUFACTURING

Marketing Processes _____

_____

_____

_____

_____

_____

_____

_____

_____

_____

Proprietary or Licensed Processes _____

_____

_____

_____

_____

_____

_____

Key Equipment and Its Technological Status _____

_____

_____

_____

_____

_____

_____

_____

Production Scheduling and Control _____

_____

_____

_____

_____

_____

Purchasing Practices _____

_____
_____
_____
_____
_____
_____
_____
_____
_____
_____

Plant Capacities (current and past levels, attach records)_____

_____
_____
_____
_____
_____
_____
_____
_____
_____
_____
_____
_____

Preventive Maintenance Programs _____

_____
_____
_____
_____
_____
_____
_____
_____

Quality Assurance Programs _____

_____

_____

_____

_____

_____

_____

_____

_____

_____

_____

_____

Past and Potential Product Liability_____

_____

_____

_____

_____

_____

_____

_____

Additional Information _____

_____

_____

_____

_____

_____

_____

_____

_____

_____

_____

_____

_____

_____

_____

Section 5.0

MANAGEMENT AND PERSONNEL

Number of Employees _____

Employee Roster (attach organizational chart)

Name	Position	Location	Compensation	Other Benefits

Employee Unions or Organizations _____

_____

_____

_____

_____

_____

_____

_____

Policy and Procedure Manuals in Use (obtain copies for review) _____

_____

_____

_____

Employee Orientation and Training _____

_____

_____

_____

_____

_____

_____

_____

_____

_____

Review of Employment Files, Records, Posters, etc. _____

_____

_____

_____

_____

_____

_____

Employee/Management Lawsuits or Claims _____

_____

_____

_____

_____

Management Style and Philosophy _____

_____

_____

_____

_____

_____

_____

_____

_____

_____

_____

_____

Remarks _____

_____

_____

_____

_____

_____

_____

_____

_____

_____

_____

_____

_____

_____

Section 6.0

FINANCIAL CONDITION AND ACCOUNTING PRACTICES

Attach Balance Sheet and Profit and Loss Statements for last three years

Comments _____

_____

_____

_____

_____

_____

_____

_____

_____

Attach Budget Forecast for Next Year, Comments _____

_____

_____

_____

_____

_____

_____

_____

Banking Relationships _____

_____

_____

CPA _____

Insurance Policies and Issues of Concern _____

_____

_____

_____

_____

Status of Accounts Payable _____

_____

Status of Accounts Receivable _____

_____

Status of Tax Payments _____

_____

_____

Tax Issues of Concern (attach last three tax returns) _____

_____

Capital Requirements for Next Three Years _____

_____

_____

_____

_____

Accounting Practices _____

_____

_____

Additional Information _____

_____

_____

_____

_____

_____

_____

_____

_____

_____

Section 7.0

COMPUTER APPLICATIONS

Computer Systems _____

_____

_____

_____

_____

_____

_____

_____

_____

_____

_____

_____

Plans for Upgrading or Extending Computer Applications _____

_____

_____

_____

Training Programs _____

_____

_____

Personnel Involved _____

_____

_____

_____

Additional Information _____

_____

_____

_____

_____

Section 8.0

LEGAL AFFAIRS

Legal Counsel _____

Lawsuits, Claims, Judgments, etc. _____

_____

_____

Past Lawsuits, Claims, Judgments, etc. _____

_____

Business Documents (contracts, leases, purchase orders, etc.) Reviewed by Legal Counsel _____

_____

Standard UCC Forms in Use _____

_____

Stock Redemptions, Purchase Options, Partnership Buy/Sells, etc., in Effect_____

_____

Outstanding Powers of Attorney _____

Plans for Ownership Transition _____

_____

Is Corporate Book Up To Date _____

Additional Information _____

_____

_____

_____

_____

Appendix VII

USEFUL FEDERAL PUBLICATIONS

Federal Trade Commission
Mall Building, Suite 500
118 St. Clair Ave.
Cleveland, OH 44114

- A Business Guide to the Mail Order Rule
- Warranties: Making Business Sense Out of Warranty Law
- Getting Business Credit
- Writing a Care Label: How to Comply with the Amended Rule
- How to Advertise Consumer Credit
- Buying a Phone Fact Sheet

Small Business Administration
P.O. Box 15434
Ft. Worth, TX 76119

- Your Business and the SBA
- Women's Handbook
- SBA PASS and Application
- Score Brochure

The SBA also has information on workshops and programs beneficial to business and much more. Call your local office for assistance.

U.S. Government Printing Office
Washington, D.C. 20402

- Patents and Inventions and Information Aid for Inventors
- General Information for Inventors
- Obtaining Information from Patents
- Questions and Answers about Patents
- Questions and Answers about Plant Patents
- Disclosure Documents Program
- General Information about Trademarks
- Questions and Answers about Trademarks

Internal Revenue Service

Contact any office

- Tax Guide for Small Business, No. 334
- Tax Withholding and Estimating Tax, No. 505
- Self-Employment Tax, No. 533
- Business Expenses and Operating Losses, No. 535
- Withholding Taxes and Reporting Requirements, No. 539
- Tax Information on Partnerships, No. 541
- Tax Information on Corporations, No. 542
- Information Returns, No. 916

Appendix VIII

SHORT LIST OF REQUIRED INFORMATION

_____ Merchandise Inventory

_____ Equipment and Fixture Inventory

_____ Equipment Leases

_____ Franchise and Licensing Agreements

_____ Building Lease (executed copy)

_____ Assignable Notes and Contracts

_____ Schedule of Accounts Receivable

_____ Schedule of Accounts Payable

_____ Corporate Resolution

_____ Profit and Loss Statements (past five years)

_____ Current Balance Sheet

_____ Real Estate Tax Bills (current year)

_____ Real Estate Deed, Title Policy, Appraisal and Survey

_____ Advertising Materials (used over past year)

_____ Insurance Policies

_____ Equipment Appraisals

_____ Union Contract

_____ _____

_____ _____

_____ _____

_____ _____

Appendix IX

AN ENTREPRENEUR'S GUIDE TO PREPARING A SUCCESSFUL BUSINESS PLAN

To the entrepreneur planning to start or purchase a new business, the preparation of a written business plan can become a major stumbling block. To many it seems to be just another troublesome exercise imposed upon them by their banker or accountant to delay their entry into business. Others just don't know where to get started, even though their plans for their business are vividly detailed in their minds.

Most would-be business owners forego the bother of preparing a written business plan and join the 80% of hopefuls that fail during their first three years in business. If you want to be different and become a successful business owner, this guide will help you through the basic planning process. Your local library will have many books entirely on business planning to provide you with more detailed guidance.

Preparing a business plan provides you with four principal benefits:

1. Planning forces you to take an objective and unemotional look at your business ideas. Through the planning process and interaction with others, you will broaden understanding of your intended business and business in general. You will be able to predict more accurately the course of your business and discover pitfalls that would have caused its failure.

2. Your completed business plan becomes an excellent communications tool that allows you to present your plans to others whose help you need in starting, buying or funding your business.

3. Your business plan (and its frequent revisions) becomes an important management tool. It will help you avoid problems and take advantage of opportunities for growth and increased profitability.

4. Your business plan will demonstrate to others that you are serious about developing a successful business and that you understand the value of continuous business planning. This will allow you to acquire more easily the business and financial support you need.

An effective business plan does not need to be fancy, but it must be clear, concise, logical and realistic. The format and content of a business plan varies with the type and size of business undertaken, but a business plan developed in accordance with the following outline should meet the needs of most businesses.

- Cover Letter

- Title Page

- Executive Summary

- Table of Contents

- Description of Company

- Market Analysis

- Marketing Plans

- Means of Production

- Purchasing Plans

- Ownership and Management

- Employees

- Financial Condition and Forecasts

COVER LETTER

Use the cover letter to introduce yourself and your business (let your enthusiasm show) and state your purpose for making contact (for example, to request financial or technical support). State how the person would benefit from assisting you with your business. The letter should be short — no longer than two pages. Conclude the letter by saying that you will call in a few days to answer any questions and discuss participation in the business.

TITLE PAGE

- Name of your company, accompanied by logo

- Term of plan (for example a three year business plan for the ABC Company)

- Effective date of plan

- Your name, address, telephone and fax number

EXECUTIVE SUMMARY

- Summarize the nature of your business — its who, what, where, how and when

- Describe how your product or services will provide the benefits desired by your target customers

- Define your competitive edge and how it will be used and maintained

- Project sales and profits over the next three years

TABLE OF CONTENTS

- Name of chapter and its opening page number

- All attachments, usually as a list of Appendices

- Bibliography

DESCRIPTION OF COMPANY

- Origin, structure, ownership and purpose of company (mission statement)

- Products and services offered and the markets to be served

- Your competitive edge, exclusive territory, unique product or service, special marketing expertise, filling gap in service, etc.

MARKET ANALYSIS

- Sales and profit history of your industry

- Major competitors and their relative marketshare

- Results of market surveys and product research

- Pricing structure and strategies

- Changes in the marketplace and how they are related to your entry into the market

- Potential barriers to competition — easy entry into market, rapid technological change, difficult exit from market, limited number of customers or suppliers, etc.

MARKETING PLANS

- Products and services to be offered

- Target market (customer profiles, buying motives, etc.)

- Pricing policies and structure (sales promotions)

- Advertising program — budget, media, message, timing

- Logo, trademarks, slogans, etc., and how they will be used

- Sales projections, based on results from marketing efforts

- Expected life cycles for products or services and actions required

- Plans for product distribution — indicate all parties involved

MEANS OF PRODUCTION (for manufacturing operations)

- Methods of production and major equipment and processes
- Age of equipment and whether it will be purchased or leased
- Availability, source and cost of raw materials
- Labor and skill levels required — cost and availability
- Production capacity and scheduling
- Inventory management
- Subcontracting to be used
- Environmental, safety and health considerations
- Quality assurance program

PURCHASING PLANS (retail and wholesale operations)

- Primary vendor and sole sources
- Vendor billing policies of vendors
- Purchasing cycle
- Inventory levels and control procedures
- Merchandise delivery and storage

OWNERSHIP AND MANAGEMENT

- Organization chart
- Resumes of key personnel
- Type and distribution of ownership and initial capitalization
- Management philosophy, style and methods

EMPLOYEES

- Number and type of employees required (include position descriptions)
- Employee classification, compensation, benefits, etc.
- Training and certification or licensing required
- Source and availability of employees

FINANCIAL CONDITION AND FORECASTS

- Financial status

- Projected sales, expenses and profits (three to five years) (present best, worst and most likely cases)

- Projected cash flow and capital requirements

- Financial forecasts

- Break-even analysis

- Use and distribution of profits

If your business plan is to make a good first impression, it should be professionally typed, copied and bound (with a plastic spiral binding or in a ring notebook with clear view front pocket for title page). Use a desktop publishing service, which can prepare professional-looking charts and graphs and facilitate easy revision. The more "visual" your plan, the more likely it is to get read and understood. Ask someone unfamiliar with your business to edit your completed business plan to be sure that it can be read and understood by those outside your industry. If possible, a professional editor should be retained to make a final review of your plan.

ABOUT THE AUTHOR

Ronald J. McGregor, is the founder and president of Michigan Management Group, Inc., a full-service consulting firm providing business origination, acquisition and expansion services to businesses throughout the Midwest. Mr. McGregor serves as an adjunct professor for the MBA program at Lake Superior State University and undergraduate business program at Ferris State University. In addition, he has developed fifteen business workshops that he teaches at eight other colleges and for individual companies.

Mr. McGregor has managed industrial development and environmental protection projects for private industry. He has a M.S. degree from Michigan Technological University and a B.S. degree from Saginaw.

NOTES

NOTES

ABOUT CRISP PUBLICATIONS

We hope that you enjoyed this book. If so, we have good news for you. This title is only one in the library of Crisp's best-selling books. Each of our books is easy to use and is obtainable at a very reasonable price.

Books are available from your distributor. A free catalog is available upon request from Crisp Publications, Inc., 1200 Hamilton Court, Menlo Park, California 94025. Phone: (415) 323-6100; Fax: (415) 323-5800.

Books are organized by general subject area.

Personal Improvement

Communications

Small Business and Financial Planning